My Psalms - Pouring My Heart Out To God Volume 2

Personal Psalms, Volume 2

Bob Skoubo

Published by Bob Skoubo, 2024.

While every precaution has been taken in the preparation of this book, the publisher assumes no responsibility for errors or omissions, or for damages resulting from the use of the information contained herein.

MY PSALMS - POURING MY HEART OUT TO GOD VOLUME 2

First edition. July 10, 2024.

ISBN: 979-8224418701

Written by Bob Skoubo.

Table of Contents

Hello, my name is Bob Skoubo. The last name is pronounced with 2 long "o's." The "u" is silent. Phonetically, the last name would look like this skŌbŌ. After all that, it really doesn't matter how it is pronounced.

I began writing psalms in 2019 when I was searching for a commentary or a study I was doing on a psalm for our small group study. I found an instruction sheet on writing psalms, and I was fascinated. I presented it to our group, and they were interested. I am probably the only one who got hooked.

This is Volume 2 of my psalms. I am hoping to get more published as the year goes by. I find that writing psalms is cathartic. It actually helps me to see myself more clearly than at other times. I do not write them to make myself feel better about myself. I have to be blatantly honest; I have to be honest in my prayers to God because He knows me better than I know myself.

I love to write psalms. I want to make a point very clear; I am <u>not</u> writing Scripture. The psalms I write are simply me pouring my heart out to God and Jesus. I do not consider them *inspired* as the Scriptures of the Bible. These psalms come from my heart as I pour out my emotions, thoughts, and desires to God.

Occasionally, I assume a persona to write a psalm. The easiest way to explain this is that I try to think and write as a person going through the experience described within.

My favorite type of psalm is one that I write for people who are dealing with various concerns in their lives. Whether it be for someone grieving for a lost loved one or someone going through treatment for a serious disease. These are very personal psalms that are written to touch the heart for encouragement in their time of difficulty.

I pray that you might find hope and encouragement reading my psalms, prayers from my heart to God our Father. I have found it very helpful in my Christian walk to write psalms.

In Christ Jesus,

Bob Skoubo

Dr. Mike Wilde and wife Susan

The Psalms are the responses of men who were inspired by God to praise and petition God in many different circumstances. How often have we found ourselves praising God as we read them while celebrating, worshiping, singing, and even crying out to Him with a broken hearts using their words as our own?

Here, Bob Skoubo writes his own "My Psalms" that reflect his praises and prayers to the Lord. They remind me of The Valley of Vision, puritan prayers and spiritual exercises written to encourage individuals and families in their own worship of God. "My Psalms, Volume 2", continue in this same vein; to worship God through the personal reflections of a follower of Jesus Christ who pours his own heart out to God through prayerful prose.

I have known Bob for years, not only as a member of our congregation but also as a good friend. I have always appreciated his personal commitment to prayer, his sincere love for God and the way he constantly offers to pray with others. When it comes to praying, there are times we find it hard to form the right words for our own petitions. It is my hope that "My Psalms" will prompt you in your own personal prayers and praises to God.

Jake Rawson, Director of Content @ LBC

I want to thank Jake Rawson who is pictured above. Jake helped me with the final design of the cover for this book. Jake is the Director of Content at Laurelwood Baptist Church in Vancouver, WA where we worship our Lord and Savior Jesus Christ.

My Psalm 101 – That Day

I need You, God,
  For I know that You are able,
  To keep that which I've committed
  Unto You against that day.
  I trust You, Lord
  And I know I am forgiven.
  I will kneel in praise before You,
  And see Your face on that day.
  Oh, that day, on that day
  When I can praise You face to face,
  And that day, yes that day,
  I long to hear You say,
  Well done good and faithful servant,
  Oh, that day, on that day.
  O LORD my God,
  I wait for that day!
  I praise You God,
  My good Father You are.
  Your mercies never fail me.
  I put my faith in You O Lord.
  You can't fail me,
  You never have and never will.
  I will praise You each day that I live,
  For eternity on that day!
  Because, Lord Jesus,
  You were the sacrifice for me.
  You bore my shame and my sin,
  To set my sinful soul free.
  Death where is your sting?
  And grave where is your victory?

You can't break the hold,
The hold that Jesus has on me!

My Psalm 102 – We Are Holy in Christ

My heart is aching for the lost,
    And my soul is aching for the sick.
    I feel the loss of the many people,
    Who have lost everything in their lives.
    I hurt for those who have lost
    Their loved ones to natural disaster.
    But Lord God I know that You are there.
    You are there with them to help.
    All they need to do is open their eyes,
    And their hearts to You and Your peace.
    You are the answer to all their hurts.
    You are the answer to all their sadness.
    I can understand the despair of the lost,
    But I can also understand it in the saved.
    Many people are realizing that living,
    Is not without trials or trying events.
    We are impatient with what we cannot control,
    We do not want to trust You, O God.
    By Your grace we are saved unto eternity,
    And by Your mercy we are forgiven.
    This is only possible because Jesus died.
    He died a horrible death on the cross for us.
    You are the Author and Perfecter of our faith.
    And You are the power behind salvation's plan.
    People like to blame You, O Lord, when pain comes.
    They cannot accept the consequence of their actions.
    Our world is filled with people who want it their way,
    And if it does not turn out right God, You are blamed.
    Man unleashes his sin into the world without thought,
    Expecting no repercussion for what they have done.

You hold the keys to hell and the path to salvation,
But most people do not want to accept it.
You are truly our good, loving Father and Lord,
And You have provided a way out of sin if we want.
You O Lord God are holy and righteous above all.
But You love us even though we are sinners.
You love us enough that You gave Jesus to die.
To die for our filthy sinful lives and souls.
Jesus loved us enough to sacrifice Himself,
And freely went to the cross knowing what would happen.
You have allowed us to become holy in Jesus,
Because we are not on our own O God!

My Psalm 103 – I Want to Give You Glory

Lord God, I want to give You glory.
> And do it in any way that I can.
> For You are holy and righteous in love
> To everyone in the world, even sinners.
> O Lord, You loved us enough to suffer
> So that we would not have to die ourselves.
> But I look at what is going on in the world,
> And I see a lot of hate and discontent growing.
> I sometimes ask You, "Where are You in all this?"
> When so many people are being hurt or worse.
> People are dying needlessly and for nothing,
> But their self-pride and hatred for You, Lord.
> But Lord You still love each one of the people,
> But You hate the sins that they are committing.
> Lord, You are willing to forgive the sinner's sins,
> If he will simply place his faith in Jesus Christ.
> It is a very simple and loving thing that You do,
> By offering salvation complete by faith in Him.
> But man cannot accept the truth that he needs You
> To become one of Your children, it's a lie to him.
> He believes that he can save himself by his goodness,
> But he is unwilling to do what is good and right.
> Man believes that he is right in all he does.
> And that he can save himself from eternal death.
> The simple and complete truth is that man is lost.
> And he cannot save himself without Jesus.
> Before time began Jesus was set to be our Lord,
> And the Savior of mankind if they would believe.

Man wants everything to be done his way,
Which eliminates Jesus and salvation in their lives.
Simply put, man cannot save himself by himself,
Because he has no righteousness of his own.
Man will continue to do what is right in his own eyes,
Until he fully accepts that he is lost without Jesus.
Lord, I despair over this fact, but I know You are holy,
And that You are just and righteous in judgement.
Lord, my despair is not because of Your holiness,
It is because of the loss these people face.
I praise You God for Who You are, for Jesus, His death,
And Your Holy Spirit and for salvation through Jesus.

My Psalm 104 – Lord, I Come to You

Lord, I come to You,
> My heart and soul in hand.
> I come humbly before You,
> For I am lost as ever.
> I feel lost, O Lord,
> For in sin, I am guilty.
> Lord, I am a sinner,
> And I need Your forgiveness.
> I know my own heart
> Finds sin most appealing.
> It may be for a season,
> Or onetime happening.
> No matter how long,
> Sin is sin, it is still sinful.
> I am afraid my Lord,
> My sin breaks Your heart.
> I do not like sin,
> But it still happens.
> I do not want to sin,
> But yet, I do, O Lord.

My Psalm 105 – Our Lord God Almighty

Lord God, these are confusing times,
    When Christians are turning against each other.
    Families are fighting against each other,
    Because they believe something different.
    Why can they not see that we all serve You,
    And that You and Your word do not change?
    Please, O Lord, help us to make things right,
    So that the world does not see all this strife.
    Only You, can touch each and every heart,
    And give us the desire to live in peace.
    Only You can give us the longing to love,
    And to be one with all our true brothers.
    I feel a deep-seated sadness within my soul,
    My heart longs for the true fellowship we had.
    It is being destroyed by people who misinterpret.
    And twist Your holy word to meet their needs.
    Many unkind and untrue things are being said,
    Because of politics rather than truth from Your word.
    Lord God, You never change, You remain the same,
    In that You love all of us, even when we commit sin.
    I praise You, for Your love and grace freely flowing,
    To all people who would truly believe in You Lord.
    Lord God, You are omniscient and omnipotent,
    And if Your will is that we should change, it will be.
    Some of us cannot see the truth through all the lies,
    That the enemy has forced upon people in this world.
    Sadly, many people who consider themselves Christians,
    Are willing to accept these lies as Your Gospel truth.
    They use Your holy word to manipulate weak believers,
    Sometimes shape them into enemies of Your truth.

Lord, please reach down and touch each one of these souls,
And help them to see Your holy truth and salvation.
Please help them to seek You first, and not the world,
And not accept what one person may say is true.
Lord, I know that if You will people to understand the truth,
It will happen and the split that we see will disappear.
It is my prayer that You can reach down and touch,
Each and every one of us Lord, so we desire to glorify You.
You alone are worthy of our praise, honor, and adoration,
For You are our Lord God Almighty.

My Psalm 106 – Despair

Lord, my heart and soul are in deep despair
    Because of something that I cannot control.
    My heart is broken because of the cutting words
    Of my own family who seem to blame me.
    My soul is in despair because of the unkind words,
    That have been spoken by those who should love me.
    Lord God, please help me through this time in life,
    That has seemed to create a separation in my family.
    Father, am I truly that much of a loser for this treatment,
    And do I deserve to be chastised by them?
    Am I so selfish and self-centered that I cannot see?
    And do I think of myself as the perfect one?
    I do not want to say anything to any of my family,
    Because of what they may say in reply to me.
    I am afraid to share my inner thoughts with them,
    Because they may think that I am crazy or stupid.
    Sadly, Lord, I do not believe that I can trust them,
    So that I can confide in them about how I feel.
    This all leads me to anger and deep frustration,
    And I am unsure who I can and should trust.
    I realize that I am nothing like Job, not half the man,
    But I feel as if I am an outcast with my own family.
    Part of me wants to leave and never come back,
    But the most important part wants to stay.
    I am deeply sorry for these feelings in my soul, Lord,
    I know that there is something better on the other side.
    I know that if my life were to end today,
    That I would be with You for all eternity.
    I ask for Your forgiveness for all these feelings,
    That I have allowed to take control of my life.

I confess that I have sinned by letting these feelings
Take precedence in a life that should glorify You.
Please cleanse me from all of my sins, O God,
And cleanse me from all my unrighteousness.
Replace my hurt and confusion with new feelings.
And make those new feelings be nothing but love,

My Psalm 107 – Only You Are Trustworthy

My Lord God,
You've never failed me.
Though I have failed You,
Seems like each and every day.
Your mercy abounds.
And Your grace cares for me.
You are holy and righteous,
I am sinful in every way.
But Your love,
Your love saved me.
You reached down to me,
And saved me from my sin.
When my sin abounds,
It is like a fiery hot brand.
It sears my soul,
Please, Lord, forgive me again.
You know me God,
I trust You God.
I do not trust myself,
Only You are trustworthy.

My Psalm 108 – My Sin or the Enemy

I often ask myself during the day,
     "Am I being attacked by the enemy?"
But I also remind myself that I sin,
And I do that all by myself, no help needed.
For I know the things I should do.
But I find that I do what I should not.
Lord God, please help me to know,
So that I can distinguish from lust or attack.
I know that my sins are forgiven through Christ,
If I remember to confess my sins and repent.
Father God, please give me the wisdom to know
When it is my self-serving lust or if it is the enemy.
I know Lord God, that sinful desires are within
Because I was born having a sinful nature.
My heart must be ready to fight the enemy.
But I often wonder am I my own enemy in this?
I want to glorify You my Lord God and Savior
But here I stand a sinful man, sometimes feeling lost.
Lord God, You are the only one I should be serving,
And not the sin that wants to control my body.
O God, I praise You, I love You and I need You,
For there is no other in the world like You Father.
You are all powerful, all knowing, and merciful,
To a sinner like me and to all who would believe.

My Psalm 109 – We Need You Now

O Lord my God,
>The world is in great turmoil.
>Also, my country.
>The sin runs rampant.
>And my home state
>Is rife with iniquity.
>Only You God, only You
>Are the answer to it all.
>Everyone one is selfish,
>Doing what they want.
>They do not care,
>About anything but themselves.
>Their love for You is weak,
>And in some have gone astray.
>Lord, we need You now,
>Only You can save us today.
>Abominations run wild,
>And love for fellow man is gone.
>Lord God, please reach down,
>And touch each and every soul.
>Replace the hearts of stone,
>And those of fiery sin and strife.
>Give them hearts of new flesh,
>So that you can change them.
>Lord God, to You belongs the glory,
>To You belong honor and praise.
>Your mercies are always new,
>And we can have them each day.
>But Lord, we as a people need You.
>We need You to come along side us.

Lord, when I am speaking of sins.
It is not just my brother or sister.
I too am guilty of sin against You,
For I am a sinner just like them.
We all need Your Son Jesus,
And salvation through His death.
I know He died for all who would believe.
And I believe but many people don't.
Lord God, make us all a miracle,
And save us from our sins, we need You.

My Psalm 110 – Lord, You Are More than Perfect

Lord, You have led me,
You have led me through my trials.
You have kept me safe,
When I had no place to turn.
Lord, You are more than perfect.
All You are is so very good to me.
I place all my trust in You.
I want to live according to Your will.
I praise You for my salvation.
I praise You for Your love and grace.
I praise You, Lord, for Your mercy,
Which is new each day.
You are my Heavenly Father.
You created all the things in this world.
You knew me before my life began,
And You drew me to Your heart.
You are Lord and God forever.
I know that You will never change.
Your holiness and righteousness are true.
And Your grace is now and forever real.

My Psalm 111 – Lord, I Trust You Completely

Lord God, I trust You completely,
> For there is no other I can turn to.
> You meet my every need not my wants,
> Because You know what is best for me.
> There is no other god but You O Lord,
> I trust You alone for all that I am.
> Lord God, I love You for You never fail,
> But though I may fail You, You can forgive.
> Lord, I know that You have a plan for me.
> And though it might not be clear now, it is good.
> Lord, I know that You are holy and righteous,
> But I am holy only through Your Son, Jesus Christ.
> Even though I am a very sinful man,
> You see me through Jesus, forgiving my sin.
> I know that I am blessed to overflowing,
> For there is no way that I can save myself.
> I know that I would be completely lost,
> But You had a plan even before I was born.
> I praise You my Lord God,
> For Your holiness and righteousness.
> I praise You for Your salvation plan,
> For without it I would be lost.
> I praise You Heavenly Father
> For Your mercies that are new every day.
> Praise You for Your lovingkindness,
> And the love You show me each and every day.
> I praise You for Your power and Your care,
> For I know that I would not be here without it.

I praise You that You have filled the void in me,
The void in my body that is shaped just like You.
I praise You God for Jesus's death on the cross,
To save me from my sins and allow me to be Your son.
I praise You, Lord, for Your Holy Spirit Who indwells me,
And is my Guide and convicts me of my sins.
I praise You, O my Lord God, and Heavenly Father
For I know, I can trust You completely.

My Psalm 112 – I Pray Because I Love My God

If you were to ask me why I pray,
    I would look at you and simply say.
    I pray because I love my God,
    I pray because He loves me too.
    I pray because I love the Lord Jesus,
    Because He died on the cross for me.
    I pray because I love my family,
    And I want them to be saved.
    I pray for my friends because I love them,
    I want them to know Jesus like I do.
    I pray for people who live around me,
    Because they need Jesus for salvation.
    I pray for people I don't even know,
    I pray for their safety and salvation of their souls.
    I pray for those who may hate me and my faith,
    I pray that God would show them the truth.
    I pray for those who are our leaders,
    For them to seek God's will and not their own.
    I pray because it is a way that I can worship God,
    And tell Him how awesome He is.
    I pray because I want to talk to God my Father,
    So that I can show my love for Him.
    I pray not to just ask God for material gain,
    I pray to let Him know how much I love Him.
    I do not pray to try to make myself look good,
    Nor do I pray flowery orations filled with pride.
    I pray because Jesus said to His disciples,
    "When you pray," He did not say "If you pray."

I pray because I feel that my Lord and God
Has put it in my heart to pray for all people.
My prayers are simply my way of talking with God,
To let Him know I am honored to be His child.
I pray to give my God thanksgiving for all He has done,
For without His salvation plan, I would not be heard.
I pray to praise my Lord God through Jesus Christ,
For all that He has done for me and all mankind.

My Psalm 113 – My Life has Changed

My trust is in You O Lord,
    And I put my trust in only You.
    I let my faith lead me, Lord.
    I can trust it in good times and bad.
    You are always with me Lord,
    You have never forsaken my trust.
    I can depend upon Your kindness,
    And I rely upon Your Holy Word.
    I trust In You Lord Jesus,
    Because You died for all my sin.
    I trust my Lord God the Father,
    Lord Jesus Christ, and Holy Spirit too.
    I praise Your Name, I praise Your love,
    And I praise You for my everything.
    You have made my life complete,
    You made me whole when I was lost.
    My life has changed, I'm different now,
    Nothing can take You away from me.
    Lord, I want to live my life for You.
    May You be seen in everything I do.
    Lord may my word be true to You.
    May they always glorify Your Name.
    Please do not let me stray,
    Because it is with You I long to stay.
    I want to reside within Your grace.
    What or where else could I even try.
    I need You Lord for I often lose my way,
    When something bad looks good.
    Your mercy and grace reach out to me,
    And You pull me out of sin's harmful way.

I cannot praise You enough, for it to be complete,
Because my words always fall short.
So, may my praises ring out for You every day,
And may they come from my very heart.
I praise You God because You are God,
My Father, the Son, and the Holy Spirit.

My Psalm 114 – Fill Me with Your Holy Word

Lord there are times Your word,
Burns within like a holy fire.
There are times that it cuts me,
Deeper than the sharpest knife.
Your word is what I cling to,
When the enemy is at my door.
Your word is oh so holy and true,
It gives me strength when I am weak.
Please dear Lord, light Your fire within,
Let it burn away all my sin.
May it heal the wounds in my heart,
That my sin would be cleansed within.
My soul longs to see You, O Lord,
From deep within I long to be with You.
For in this world my desires may not be holy,
Because it is a hateful, unholy place.
Within my body I know that sin can grow,
Without You Lord it would take control.
O Lord, You are so holy and righteous,
And I can never in this life be like You.
I have no righteousness on my own Lord,
My righteousness comes from Jesus Christ.
I know He died to save my soul from my sin,
And without Him in my life I'd be lost for eternity.
Lord, please light that holy fire in me,
Make it burn out all the traces of sin.
May Your holy word be with me forever,
Please write it upon the walls of my heart.

I praise You, Father for Your Son,
And I praise You for Your Holy Spirit.
You have changed my heart, You changed my soul,
Now I want to live for You alone.
You made my life complete when You came in,
And I do not want to ever go back again.

My Psalm 115 – Lord, My Heart Longs for You

Lord, my heart longs for You,
I desire in my heart to be with You.
I want to see You face to face,
I want to see You smile on me.
My soul's desire is to worship You,
And I long to praise You as I see You.
For You are my Lord and my God,
And You are my only God and Savior.
Your holiness and righteousness never pale,
And Your mercies will never fail me.
O Lord God, my Heavenly Father, I love You,
I praise You for Your Son's death for my sin.
There is no other god who is worthy,
Is worthy of all our praise O Lord.
I pray that my praise will be without end,
And that my love for You will never cease.
I want to glorify You to the lost of the world,
Because of all that You have done for all of us.
Father, your magnificent grace has come to all,
I will not refuse it though many others do.
I praise You, Father, for Your Son Jesus Christ.
I know that You love us enough to sacrifice Him for us.
Lord God, may my praises never fail to reach Your ears,
And may my thankfulness for Your salvation never end.
You, Lord God, are my Father in heaven,
You loved me even before I knew that You were real.
Jesus Christ, You gave Yourself, Your life, up for me,
While I was dead and lost in my vile and ugly sin.
You, Holy Spirit, I praise You for being part of my life,
I need Your care and guidance every step of my way.

O Lord God, Heavenly Father, I love You, my Lord,
And my heart longs for You, O Lord God, my God.

My Psalm 116 – Can I Be a Blessing?

Lord, I try hard to be kind to everyone,
    And I do try hard to glorify You, Lord.
    I try to create a relationship with people,
    So that I can confidently share Your grace.
    My heart's desire is to see them come to You,
    For I would like to see them in eternity.
    Sometimes I fail more than miserably,
    Because I try to do it all on my own.
    I have come to love the people that I know.
    I truly seek to share Your word with them.
    I want them to know how blessed I am.
    I would like them to be blessed as I am.
    Lord God, please help me to share Your love,
    Your grace, Your majesty, and Your mercies.
    Please help me to share You and not me.
    I want them to see You in me and my life.
    I am afraid that they may think badly of me,
    If I truly share my beliefs and faith with them.
    Lord God, how can I be a blessing to people,
    When I stumble over myself when I try?
    Lord, can I be a blessing to them if I am there?
    Must I go out of my way to comfort them?
    Lord, is my testimony about You enough,
    To help them to understand my faith in You?
    Lord, please as the old hymn says so well,
    Make me a blessing and make me one today.
    Lord, please give me the heart I need to do this.
    Please help my life to be a blessing to one and all.
    Please, Lord, can I be a blessing today to everyone,
    And let it be for Your glorification alone, not mine.

My Psalm 117 – For You, Jesus, are Lord

Come now O my soul,
 Come and praise our Lord.
 See now O my heart,
 For He is worthy of praise.
 Be humble O my soul,
 And fear the Lord God.
 For You O Lord my God,
 Are gracious and loving.
 God, You are my Lord,
 And You are my Savior.
 Your only Son died for me,
 To save me from my sin.
 With my heart I praise You,
 O Lord Jesus Christ, my Savior.
 For You Lord saved me,
 You are worthy of my praise.
 You bought eternity for me,
 When You died at Calvary.
 I love You Lord Jesus,
 And I need You even more.
 I want You in my life,
 For You have lifted me.
 Your death bought my life,
 Secured me eternally, O Lord.
 Come now O my soul,
 Let us rejoice in our Lord.
 Come now O my heart,
 And see that He is good.
 Come now O my life,
 To be lived for Him alone.

Lord Jesus, my life is Yours,
And my soul is Yours too.
May I always praise You,
In the good times and bad.
May my love grow stronger,
For You, Jesus, are Lord.

My Psalm 118 – Lord God, My Heart Aches

Lord God, my heart aches,
    And my soul is deeply saddened.
    I see people not following You Lord,
    They do what is right in their own eyes.
    They know the commandments from You,
    But they choose to have their ears tickled.
    I know that I could have the same tendency,
    If I were to turn from You but I know better,
    Because I know that I too am a sinner.
    My sins are just as filthy dirty as theirs,
    But I seek to do Your will my Lord God.
    For You have set everything in motion,
    And You have put our leaders before us.
    You established our government for us,
    We are to obey them because You said.
    Many are rebelling for the wrong reason,
    And they are not looking to do Your will.
    Lord, please do not hold it against them,
    But show them Your will for their lives.
    Please help them to see the truth,
    Open their eyes to the truth in Your word.
    Though we may not agree with our leaders,
    Does not mean that we should rebel.
    Lord, through Your holy word, show them,
    Open their eyes and hearts to the truth.
    Lord, You are the only One who can do it,
    For they can be stubborn in heart and mind.
    Many ignore the truth of Your word,

For they are too set in their ways to listen.
Lord, my heart breaks for those people,
Because they are my brothers and sisters.
I love them because they are a part of my family,
We are related through Jesus's shed blood.
I will continue to pray for them Lord God,
Praying that they will return to doing Your will.

My Psalm 119 – My Soul Cries from My Sin

O LORD God, I am nothing but a sinner,
    I am sinful even though I do not want to be.
    My sinful nature desires things of the flesh,
    And I am appalled that I allowed it to win.
    My soul cries because of my sinfulness,
    And I know that my sin glorifies You not.
    Lord God, You alone are holy and righteous,
    Your desires for man are pure and holy.
    Your being God means that all Your thoughts,
    All Your desires for my life are based on holiness.
    You chastise me in different ways when I sin,
    By showing me what I have done is wrong.
    I tend to turn away from You, my Lord God,
    Because I let the sin that I live in control me.
    In my heart, I know that my sins are wrong,
    But my lust for pleasure leads me there.
    I am ashamed of the sinful things that I do,
    For they are of no value to my soul or to You Father.
    Please help me to find the strength and will,
    To overcome my sinful desires that control me.
    I do not want to sin, I want to glorify You,
    I want to praise Your name, Lord God, and overcome.
    Yet my soul cries out and my heart, it does ache,
    Because I know that each of my sins grieves You Lord.
    My desire is to be like You, my Lord God,
    Because You saved me from my sin and eternal death.
    My heart and soul ache, longing for Your holiness,
    Because I sinned against You and broke our fellowship.

I want to be right with You Lord God,
And I want nothing to come between us.
I confess to You Lord God and Heavenly Father,
I am a sinful man who allows sin reign at times.
I come to You Lord God, for my sins are very great.
My heart melts inside of me knowing I have hurt You.
Lord, please help me to cast off my sinfulness,
And to stand only for You through Jesus Christ.
For I know that the only way I can be holy or righteous,
Is through Your only Son, my Savior, Jesus Christ.

My Psalm 120 – I Can Praise You O Lord at any Time

I can praise You O Lord at any time,
    And I can sing of my love for You too.
    I love You Lord because You are my Father.
    I need You Lord because Jesus is my Savior.
    O Lord, You are most holy and righteous,
    And there is none like You, my Lord God.
    I will praise You in the morning with my voice,
    I will praise You in the afternoon loudly.
    I can praise You in the evening for Your love,
    And I can praise You for Your Creation.
    There is nothing that can stop my praise for You,
    Nothing in life, even my death, or another person.
    My love for You cannot compare with Yours for me,
    But I do wish that mine could be so much stronger.
    My love for You pales in the light of Your love so strong,
    Because my love wavers because of sin in my life.
    I pray that my faith and love is strong enough,
    To even suffer death because I believe in Your word.
    Lord Your love means You will not let me down,
    As friends and family have done over the years.
    You love me enough to not give in to my wants.
    Your love is so strong that You give me what I need.
    You are aware that my needs outweigh my wants,
    And You love to give me exactly what I need.
    Lord God, I praise You for Your holy power.
    I praise You for Your Creation where I live.
    I praise You because You made all things fit perfectly,
    For You are the perfect Designer and Creator.

I praise You for my salvation through Jesus Christ,
And I praise You for Your Holy Spirit, Who is my guide.
I praise You for being my loving, holy, Heavenly Father,
I praise You for allowing me to be Your child.

My Psalm 121 – Sing Praises to Your Name

You are my Lord God,
>My Father and my Friend.
>I put my faith in You,
>I trust no other but You.
>You carried me in my weakness,
>Gave me courage in fear.
>No one is Your equal.
>You love me just as I am.
>Your grace cut through my sin.
>Jesus's shed blood cleansed me.
>God in Your holiness and love,
>You have set my soul free.
>I praise You and I love You,
>Because You loved me first.
>Like a thirsty man I do long,
>For Your Spirit to quench my thirst.
>You are my Savior,
>My Provider and my stay.
>There is not another,
>To save me for that day.
>I long to be with You Lord,
>To see You face to face.
>To bow in Your presence,
>And sing praises to Your Name!

My Psalm 122 – God, You are Most Beautiful

With my soul I praise You O Lord,
    With my voice I will shout Your praises.
    My heart will praise You with each beat.
    My eyes will behold Your glory in creation.
    I will sing praises to Your holy name Lord God,
    And my praises will never end, no matter what.
    You are worthy of all my praise and worship,
    For You are the Lord God of all the universe.
    As Jesus Himself said, "Only God is good,
    And You are holy and righteous beyond compare.
    You are Creator, Lord, and Holy Father,
    And You love us enough to provide us salvation.
    You are my God, My Lord, and my Savior,
    You created a plan by which men could be saved.
    Your only Son came to earth to live as a man.
    He was not like us because He was sin free.
    He was and is our Lord and Savior,
    And He is one with God the Father.
    I long to be with You O Lord God, Heavenly Father,
    I desire to see Jesus face to face and praise Him.
    I fear that my sin might separate me from You,
    But I claim the promises of Your Holy Word,
    I know my fear is baseless because of Your grace,
    And I know that Your mercies are new every day.
    You are the only holy and righteous God,
    You are all powerful, all loving and filled with grace.
    Though I have never seen You O LORD God,
    I know that You are most beautiful in every way.

I eagerly wait for that day when I can praise You,
And glorify You in both word and song, face to face.

My Psalm 123 – I Need to Praise You, O LORD

Lord, a sadness has come upon me,
    I feel as though much has been lost.
    I know that I have done something,
    That has caused this feeling to be born.
    Please help me to overcome this sadness,
    And to give You the glory and the praise.
    I know that this sadness is not from You,
    But it is something coming from my soul.
    I need Your Holy Spirit to lead me through,
    To open my eyes to see why this is happening.
    My heart feels like it has been broken,
    But my soul cries out for peace, not pain.
    Lord God, I know that You are the Creator.
    You are my God and Heavenly Father,
    You are holy and righteous, and I am a sinner,
    Who can never attain holiness on my own.
    Even though I believe in Jesus as my Savior,
    What I am that is holy and righteous is from Him.
    Lord my God, I praise You for Jesus,
    And I praise You for Your Holy Spirit!
    I praise You for Your grace and mercy,
    Otherwise, I cannot approach You.
    You are holy and righteous beyond measure,
    And Your love, grace, and mercies abound.
    For I realize that my thoughts lead me astray,
    And my desire to sin can be very strong indeed.
    I try to shift my thoughts to You Lord God.
    I try to remember the cross on which Jesus died.

When these times come, I need to praise You, O Lord,
And make the cross of Jesus my focus.

My Psalm 124 – I Am Tempted to Roam

O Lord God, I am tempted to roam,
> For I let my mind stray from purity.
> Lord, I know that my thoughts stray,
> And I need to take them captive.
> At times I feel almost as if I am consumed,
> By the inappropriate thoughts in my mind.
> I need to give them to You Lord Jesus.
> I confess that those thoughts are wrong.
> They do not glorify You in any way,
> For I know that they can lead me astray.
> Lord, my thoughts are not Your thoughts.
> I want my thoughts to be about You.
> I praise You Lord God and I love You,
> For there is no other God like You.
> For You are the only true God and Father.
> You are my Creator and my Heavenly Father.
> I want to glorify You with my voice, Jesus,
> And I want my life to be all about You.
> But I sometimes let my weakness have control,
> And in my weakness, I am very apt to sin.
> I give my life and my soul to You O Lord,
> For I am too easily set out of control.
> I put my trust in You alone Jesus my Lord,
> Because You overcame the world Yourself.
> Lord God, my Father and Jesus, God the Son,
> And God the Holy Spirit, You are worthy of praise!
> For You are still on the throne of the universe,
> And You are on the throne of my heart.
> I ask that You forgive me, and my praises be heard,
> For You are the only true God, three in one.

My Psalm 125 – You Saved Me, a Wretched Man

All my praise belongs to You, O Lord.
All my faith is in You Father God.
My soul praises You from within.
My voice and actions praise You aloud.
My heart and soul belong to You Lord,
For You are the only Savior of my life.
You created the heavens and the earth.
You created me to live for You for eternity.
The heavens and the earth speak Your Name,
Because You are the One Who made them.
All praise and honor and glory are Yours alone.
Not only are You our Creator; You are our Keeper.
I place my faith in none other than You God,
Because all others are manmade and powerless.
I know dear Lord that You are all powerful.
You are gracious to sinners such as me.
Only You, O Lord God, can save my sinful soul,
Through the death and resurrection of Jesus Christ.
You are able to meet my needs before I know them,
Because You know what I need beforehand.
You are worthy of my love, praise, and honor,
Above all else and anything man has made.
You had a plan for the salvation of all true believers,
Even before man walked upon Your earth.
I am but a worm, a very wretched man.
Among men I am not esteemed or even liked.
I am not afraid of what a man might do to me,
But Lord God, I do not want to make You angry.

I confess that I am but a very sinful man.
I cannot do anything to save myself, Lord.
Jesus, I know that You are my Lord and Savior,
And that You bore my sins upon the cross.
You, Who knew no sin in Your body while here,
Became the bearer of my sins when You died.
I praise You, Lord Jesus, for all that You have done,
For You accomplished eternal life for me.

My Psalm 126 – In Times of Strife

Lord God, I find myself in times of strife,
    Asking You, "Why is this happening to me?"
    You know Lord, that I am not angry with You.
    I sometimes wonder what I did to deserve this.
    I catch myself thinking, "Am I being chastised?"
    Or are You actually pruning me for more fruit?
    Father, I know that You love me in spite of my sin,
    Because You said You would cleanse me if I confessed.
    Father God, I know that You do truly love me,
    For You sent Your Son Jesus Christ to die for my sin.
    Even when I am weak and fall into temptation,
    You are willing to continue to love me just as much.
    Lord God, I know there are a lot of sins that I allow.
    I allow it to have a temporary place in my life.
    That sin may be for a day or maybe a season,
    But it does not matter how long it lasts, it is still sin.
    I hate the sin that I commit because it grieves You.
    And I hate that fact that I have hurt and disappointed You.
    O Lord, God, and Heavenly Father, I do confess that I sin,
    Because I do not want to have You not hear my prayers.
    I know, O Lord, that You would not hear the Jews' prayers,
    Because of the sin that they committed against You.
    I praise You, Abba, Father for all Your promises.
    And I praise You that my confession will cleanse me.
    O Lord God, let my praises echo across the heavens,
    May I be bold in praising You no matter when or where.
    Father, I praise You for my salvation through Jesus.
    And I praise You that His death made me acceptable.
    For I know that without Jesus's death I would be lost,
    And lost to the eternal flames where sinners are damned.

I love You, O Lord, for Your mercies are new every morning,
And I praise You that I can stand on Your promises.
I need You Lord, for without You I am nothing in life,
For my life is but a vapor anyway, worthless without You.
I want You, O Lord God, for You are my Heavenly Father.
I need You Jesus, my Lord, and my Savior.
I need You Holy Spirit to be my guide and to intercede for me.
And I pray that You will be with me all my days in life.
You are worthy of all my praise, glorification, and honor,
God my Father, God the Son, and God the Holy Spirit.

My Psalm 127 – You Knew that I Needed Salvation

Sometimes in my mind, O Lord,
My thoughts ask, "Where are You?"
My prayers seem to be endless words,
Strung out in meaningless phrases.
Is my heart longing for Your voice?
All that I hear is the beating of my heart.
I know that You have not left me.
I know that You have not forsaken me.
I know that You promised to never leave me.
And I know that You are right here beside me.
I believe in my heart and mind that it is me.
I have a sin or sins that I have not confessed.
Lord God, You have never left me alone,
And know that You never will do that.
I trust You Lord for all that I am and will be.
I trust Your word and Your promises for my life.
You have never ceased to be my God and Father.
For You will never forsake Your holy promises.
The truth be known, I have forsaken You many times.
And I realize that You might be preparing me.
You may be pruning me or chastising me,
To help me be a better child of Yours.
Although the despair that I feel is difficult,
I know that I will come out better for it.
I praise You, Lord God for You are good,
You are holy and righteous, You are merciful.
I praise You for Your holy power, and grace.
And I praise You for my salvation and my life.

You knew me before I knew about You,
And You knew that I needed salvation.

My Psalm 128 – Jesus, You Turned Me Around

Jesus, You turned me around,
When I was headed for hell.
Everything that I wanted was easy.
It made me feel so good, so strong.
But I finally realized that it was temporal,
As soon as it was gone I wanted more.
Jesus, You turned me around to love You.
Jesus, You are forever, forever eternal.
I do not have to seek for more of You.
You are always there giving me more.
Jesus, Your Spirit urges me to grow,
And I grow more into You and You in me.
I learned and I found out that I need You.
I do not need the things of the world.
I need You more than food and water.
I want You more than anything of the world.
I love You, Jesus, You turned me around,
There is no one and nothing like You.
Jesus, You took my guilt away forever,
By dying on the cross in my place.
You bore all of my sins and the sins of the world,
Not because You were forced to, but You loved us.
Lord, Jesus, Your love for us is uncontainable,
It cannot be contained by anything made by man.
I praise You, Lord Jesus, for Your endless love.
I praise You, Father God, for Your boundless grace.
I praise You for Your Holy Spirit, Who indwells me.
I praise You for loving me, the wretch that I am.

You turned me around and You are my Lord.
You are my Savior, my Father, and my Holy Guide.
I am nothing without You, but a lost sinful man,
And I know that there is no way I can save myself.
My life was worthless without You, Jesus.
For I was living for myself and living for pleasure.
I want You in my life always because I do need You.
For Jesus, You turned me around, around to true life.

My Psalm 129 – My Pride Gets in the Way

Lord, my pride gets in the way,
For it seems to raise issues often.
My pride does not let me admit,
That sometimes I am very jealous.
My pride will not let me admit I'm wrong,
When it is obvious even to me.
Lord Jesus, I do not like myself this way,
For it allows me to hurt others.
If I am willing to let my pride hurt others,
I know that it is hurting me as well.
Jesus, my Lord, and Savior I do not like this.
I love You but I find it hard to love others.
I want to glorify You, my Lord God.
I do not want to make others think badly of You.
You are my holy and righteous Father.
I need You in my life every minute of the day.
I want to glorify You Father, and You Jesus,
And I want to glorify You Holy Spirt as well.
My life needs to be centered on You, O Lord,
Not on my selfish and self-glorifying pride.
I commit my selfish pride unto You my Lord,
Because I cannot continue to live this way.
I only hurt those who I love the most.
It makes my faith look like it is a lie.
For You are most holy and righteous,
God my Heavenly Father and Creator.
Jesus, You are wholly God and Savior.
You loved me enough to die for my sins.

Holy Spirit You are my intercessor with God.
You convict me of my sins, my pride.
I praise You Lord God and Heavenly Father.
Thank You for Your mercies new each day.
I praise You for Your love and sacrifice for me.
And I love You more than anything of this world.
I praise You Holy Spirit for living inside of me.
And guiding me to be more holy and righteous.

My Psalm 130 – I Trust You God, for You are Able

I look at the world around me,
    I see anger, hate, and murder.
    I feel my body beginning to tremble,
    But Your loving peace takes over.
    I can see the enemy at work,
    Wreaking havoc wherever he can.
    But Lord God, I know that You are here.
    And You are still sitting on Your throne.
    I trust You God, for I know you are able,
    To keep that which I've committed to You.
    Father, I need You in my life each minute,
    And every hour of these dangerous days.
    If fear tries to overcome me, I look to You.
    You know what is happening everywhere.
    Fear has no place in my life, You are in charge.
    And I trust You with my whole life, Lord God.
    For Father God, You created this world,
    And You created me to worship You.
    My heart and my spirit adore You Father.
    And I honor Your holiness and righteousness.
    I am righteous and holy because of Jesus.
    I have none apart from Him, my Savior.
    Because of this, I can do nothing but love You,
    And keep on loving You until I come home.
    Lord, I ask that my faith will be strong,
    Strong enough to even to face death itself.
    I do not fear death, though it might come,
    Because I know that I am Your child.

I believe the promises You made in Your word.
And I know physical death begins life anew.
I praise You Lord Jesus that You died for me,
And all who would put their faith in You.
You are the only means of salvation we have,
For the promises of the world are void, empty.
I praise You Father for Your plan of salvation,
Because it is true salvation that we cannot deny.
I praise You God for sacrificing Your only Son,
So that we can come to You for all eternity.

My Psalm 131 – Jesus Made Me Whole

Lost in sin and death,
    I had no hope for life.
    All I could see was sorrow,
    All I could feel was numbness.
    Sin offered me no hope,
    And my life was sad upon sad.
    I had never learned to live,
    Because I did not have Jesus.
    He came to me when He was needed,
    And replaced death with eternal life.
    The God shaped void in my soul,
    Was filled by my Lord and Savior.
    Where there was cold and bitterness,
    And sadness that I could not shake.
    Jesus came and filled me with love,
    A love that will not die or grow old.
    My life is different now because of Him,
    Jesus made me whole and gave me love.
    Jesus's Spirit gave me new life and hope.
    He did not withhold anything from me.
    The Spirit replaced the heart of stone,
    With a living beating heart of flesh.
    For Lord Jesus, my life I live for You.
    My praises I lift up in Your name only.

My Psalm 132 – Praise the Father and Son for Our Salvation

You walked the earth as a man,
Yet You were still fully God,
You became flesh and blood,
Faced the same temptations as we.
You showed Your love for man,
When You laid down Your life for us.
O Lord God, our Heavenly Father,
Thank You for sending Jesus to die.
Praise You Holy Father, You loved us,
Enough to sacrifice Your Son on the cross.
Thank You Father for paying my debt,
With the blood of Your very own Son.
Praise You Jesus for Your salvation.
Salvation bought with Your own life.
Praise You for loving us so very much,
That You suffered such deep humiliation.
I praise Your Holy Name, Lord Jesus!
You could have said, "No," but You did not.
I cannot imagine all the pain You felt,
And not just the physical pain of it all.
To have Your very own Father turn away,
Because He could not see the sin You became.
You bore our sins to death on the cross,
You won eternal life and salvation for us.
Your lifeless body rested in a cold dark tomb
For three days it was there until a spark.
That spark brought life back to Your body,
And You arose to secure our salvation.

You came to life in the power and the glory,
That we have come to know in You.
Jesus, thank You for dying in my place,
And making this wretched sinner clean.
I praise the day You arose from the dead,
For You gave me the life I'd never known.
I praise You Father, Son, and Holy Spirit,
For my life is complete in You, the Godhead.

My Psalm 133 – Jesus, None Other Can Save

O Lord, God, at times I do not understand,
How You can love mankind so much,
We are really our own worst enemies,
Because we turn away from You and Jesus.
Many do not turn away at hearing Your Name.
They run as fast as they can to escape You.
Why is it that man has hardened his heart,
And used Your Name for unholy purposes?
It seems easy to blame You for their problems,
Especially when they do not even know You.
They believe that all should be given to them,
Free and on a silver platter and be free of trusting You.
It is man who causes most of his own problems,
And You wait patiently for him to come to You.
All mankind is born under the bondage of sin,
But only You can break those chains man loves.
If only they could understand that it is sin,
And our stubbornness hat keeps us from You.
The gospel message is so simple and true,
That mankind does not want to believe in You.
We seem to get the idea we alone can do it,
When in our hearts we know that we really cannot.
It is too easy to reject the free offer of salvation,
Because we want to be in complete control.
I praise You Father for Your love and grace,
That You extended to a wretched sinner like me.
I praise You Father for sending Jesus to die for me,
To bear the weight of my sins when He died.

I praise You that all who want to believe,
Can have this eternal gift free of any charge.
For I know, O Lord God, I would be totally lost.
Lost for eternity if not for Jesus holy sacrifice.
It took His holiness and His sinless life on earth,
To be the worthy sacrifice for the sins of mankind.
I now know that I am absolutely nothing myself,
But I am saved by the shed blood of Jesus Christ.
In Him alone can I find salvation and eternity,
For none other but Jesus can save a sinner like me.

My Psalm 134 – Invest Your Soul for Eternity

The earth cries out,
    The heavens glorify!
    The rocks sing praises,
    And salvation rings forth.
    It comes full circle,
    All round the earth.
    For our God is our Lord,
    His salvation is for eternity!
    It is not bought or earned.
    We only have to believe.
    Christ claimed the victory,
    When He died on Calvary.
    No other name can save,
    But the Holy Name Jesus!
    No other can come close,
    For Jesus bore all our sins!
    Salvation comes in one name,
    That name is Jesus Christ!
    Though man may try himself,
    There is no way to be saved.
    For the gates of Hell swing wide,
    For those in the second death died.
    Salvation cannot be found in things.
    The only true salvation is Jesus!
    We cannot talk ourselves into it.
    Heaven is reserved for believers.
    Faith is the one true answer for all.
    Faith in Jesus Christ is the way.

Jesus said "I am the Way, the Truth,
And I am the life," so believe in Him!
For "No one comes to the Father,
Except through Me!" So, believe!
You cannot save your own soul,
But Jesus can save it for eternity!
Put you full trust in Him right now,
Invest your soul for eternity.

My Psalm 135 – My Heart Rejoices in You Lord

My heart rejoices in You Lord.
  I bow humbly before You, God.
  I sing praises for Your glory and grace,
  For You are loving and so kind.
  God, You love me even though I sin,
  And You forgive me through Jesus.
  I know You love me; You word says so.
  I know that You sent Jesus to die for me.
  Your word says that Jesus died for my sin,
  And the sin of the whole world to save us.
  You sent Jesus to secure our salvation,
  Because You wanted us to be with You.
  My mere words of praise are not enough,
  To express my love and faith in You Lord.
  I am but a small grain of sand in this world,
  And I do not know how to best praise You.
  May the words coming from my heart be all.
  May they be what shows my love and faith.
  Lord, God, You know that I am not holy.
  On my own I am lost, but not in Jesus Christ.
  The holiness that is in me is not my own.
  My holiness comes only from Jesus Himself.
  I praise You Lord God that I can be holy,
  Because of my faith in one person, Jesus Christ.
  You are worthy of all my praise and honor,
  For You O Lord are the Most High God.
  There is no other god before or after You.
  All other so-called gods are of man's creation.

Father You are all powerful to save us.
You are the one who created all of mankind.

My Psalm 136 – I See a Cross Upon a Hill

I see a cross upon a hill,
    Stained with blood.
    My guilty heart stands still,
    Because my sin put Him there.
    I feel my shame rising up.
    I should be the one up there.
    But Jesus freely gave Himself,
    To be a sacrifice for me.
    He knew the purpose of His life.
    He became sin's holy sacrifice.
    Jesus became sin for me,
    And bore my sins to His grave.
    But praise God for His infinite grace,
    Because Jesus rose from the dead.
    That glorious morning, He arose.
    Salvation's plan came in full bloom.
    For Jesus became sin in our place,
    So, death had no power over us.
    Now we can praise the Lord our God,
    For He had a plan to save our souls.
    Jesus died for us that we might live,
    That our lives would be for eternity.
    This salvation plan is for all.
    For we are saved from sin's fatal fall.
    Praise God that Jesus died for us,
    And we can be saved if we believe.
    Salvation's plan is simple indeed,
    But many choose to not believe.
    Place your faith in Christ alone,
    So that death will reap defeat.

Jesus died that we all might live.
He loved us enough to die for us.
For salvation comes from no other god.
Salvation is in Jesus Christ alone.
On Calvary the blood and water flowed,
To pay the debt that we alone owed.

My Psalm 137 – Please Use Me

O Lord, I have had a lot of pain,
    And it can get the best of me at times.
    Please understand I am not complaining.
    I just want You to know how I feel.
    Although I let it get ahead of me occasionally,
    I can overcome the pain with Your help.
    I do not want my pain to be an excuse,
    For I want to be true to Your calling.
    I want to glorify You, my Lord God.
    And revel in Your love, grace, and majesty.
    I know that You did not cause my pain.
    I know that it is because of my self-will.
    Please Lord, I do not want to be caught,
    Feeling sorry for the pain I've caused myself.
    I know that You can use it as a witness.
    And that I can lift Your Name on high to others.
    I do not want to be caught saying, "Why me?"
    But I want to say O Lord, "Please use me!"
    In those times that I give pain control,
    I know that I am not fully trusting You.
    Part of me wants to be pitied for the pain,
    But another part wants to praise You, O Lord!
    Here and now, I state that my life is not just pain,

    But when this life is over You still remain, Lord.

Though pain is an everyday part of my life,
I have You to look to for all that I need each day.
I praise You even through my every pain.
And I praise You for each of my daily blessings.

I do not know if this is right or if it is wrong,
But I feel the need to praise You because of pain.
You can use my pain to Your glory if You choose,
Or You could miraculously remove it from me.
I know myself though, O Lord God, Heavenly Father,
Without the pain I may not be true to You.
I praise You Lord when I am wrapped in pain,
For only You can know how I truly feel my Lord God.

My Psalm 138 – You Love Me O Lord

I can hear a still small voice, as a wind,
    Calling inaudibly for me to just follow.
    In my heart I know it is the Lord,
    Calling me to trust Him more.
    Although no one else can hear it,
    The message comes soft and clear.
    Trust Me, I am your Lord and God.
    I am your Salvation and Solid Rock.
    I saved your soul from the pit of hell.
    I am with you always and forever.
    Put your full faith in Me, the true God.
    Trust your life to Jesus Christ, my Son.
    I want to follow this loving voice,
    For I know that alone is the truth.
    A part of me says wait, it's not for you.
    It is simply your imagination tricking you.
    But I do truly believe that it is You Lord.
    I will follow You wherever I must go.
    You, O Lord God, have saved my soul.
    You have made me Your own child.
    I have You for all eternity in my heart.
    I have You always in my soul, for life.
    I trust that You sacrificed Your life,
    So that I could live for eternity.
    My faith is in You alone Christ, my Lord,
    For I know in Whom my eternity is safe.
    For there is no other name which can save,
    But that of Jesus Christ, my Lord and Savior.
    Praise You Father, praise You, Jesus Christ,
    And praise You, Holy Spirit for I am Yours.

May my life be lived just for You, Lord God,
And may it always be about glorifying You.
May my first thought in the morning be You,
So that I never forget to praise You.
I praise You, O Lord God, that You love me,
You love me enough to make me Your child.

My Psalm 139 – Call to Prayer

There is a baby so helpless,
    And his mama is fraught with tears.
    His daddy is beside himself,
    His heart filled with fear.
    He is their lovely, beloved child,
    For only a few days he's been here.
    Lord, let this be my call to praise You,
    To glorify Your holy name.
    Lord, let this be my call to worship You,
    To show my love for You, my God.
    Lord, let this be my call to prayer.
    Please hear my words, I know You care.
    I know You are the one and only Healer.
    And You make all things work together.
    I know that You hear the weeping mother.
    And I know You have counted her tears.
    You hear the prayers of the child's father,
    And You weigh each word that he says.
    Lord, God I know that You can hear us.
    We have answered this call to prayer.
    We praise You, God, our Heavenly Father,
    For we know that You truly do care.
    Please draw Your children close to You.
    As we have answered this call to prayer.
    Our desire is the same as his mom and dad.
    We pray that You will show him mercy.
    Please show the parents You do love them.
    Help them to know the child is in Your hands.
    May Your healing power reach down to him,
    And restore his life back to completeness.

Lord, I answer this call to say that "I love You,
And I trust that Your will shall be done.
Lord may our words be sweet like honey.
Sweet to Your ears showing that we care.
May our praises glorify Your holy name,
As we answer Your call for prayer.

My Psalm 140 – You Are the Best of Fathers

Please hear me O God.
>My heart is in Your hands.
>I need You now O Lord.
>My life is in Your hands.
>I am lost in my fears Lord.
>I am anxious for Your help.
>You are my Lord and my God,
>For there is none like You.
>You supply everything I need,
>But there are times I need more.
>But You know my needs better,
>For You knew me before birth.
>Lord God, I feel that I have failed.
>I have failed You through my sins.
>Jesus, I know that at times my loss,
>Is almost as if I have lost my Lord.
>I fear that my needs are not needs,
>But they are sadly only my wants.
>I trust You, O Lord God, You are worthy.
>And You are more stable than anyone.
>Through You, all of Creation is held.
>It is held together by Your infinite power.
>You created man for fellowship with You,
>But many of us turn from Your love.
>How can I ever repay You, Lord God,
>I am not rich or financially powerful.
>I know that I cannot out give You,
>For You provide all needed things.

You meet all the needs we can have,
But You do not give more than we manage.
I praise You, O Lord God, for everything,
That which You do provide for my family.
I praise You, Lord, that You do not over-provide,
So that I do not get fat, lazy and unrepentant.
I praise You, Father, Son, and Holy Spirit,
For You know me better than I know myself.
You are holy and righteous Lord God,
And You are the best of Fathers we can have.

My Psalm 141 – Your Beauty is Beyond Compare

Your beauty is beyond all else.
 There is none that could compare.
 I have not seen You face to face,
 But I know that You are by Your grace.
 Your holiness and righteousness prove,
 You are loving and merciful to us.
 God, my Heavenly Father, I need You.
 I love You and I want You in my life.
 I praise You for unwavering faithfulness.
 You cannot let me down and never will.
 Again, O Lord God, You are so beautiful,
 That no one can describe You.
 Your beauty is described in all of Creation,
 By the beauty that You provided for us.
 We cannot see You face to face right now,
 But all of Creation speaks again to Your love.
 We can love You our Heavenly Father,
 Because You loved us before time began.
 Our love for You can grow each day,
 For Your mercies are new every morning.
 Your grace is always there for us, O Lord.
 So, we desire to praise You every day.
 Lord God, we want You, we need You,
 For there is no other god but You.

My Psalm 142 – May We Praise You in Our Pain

I see pain all around me, Father.
Not just the worldly ones suffer.
I see many of my brothers in pain,
Gripped in agony that tires the soul.
My sisters in Christ have much pain.
They too are struggling to keep going.
I do not know the reason for this,
But I do not blame You Father God.
Christ promised us struggles in life,
And this struggle is just one example.
Though we struggle with pain daily.
You know what we are going through.
We all go through seasons of pain,
But those seasons are each different.
For You have given each of us a measure.
A measure of faith that can be strong.
Our faith in Jesus Christ can grow stronger,
With each day that we live if we try.
Lord God, You are to be praised,
No matter what is happening in our lives.
You know that our pain can help us grow,
Especially if we let You have full control.
O Lord God, please help us to grow,
In our pain and through our struggles.
Give us the strength to face each day,
With a new resolve and faith even stronger.
May we praise You for our pain,
And may we praise You in our pain.

Let our pain and weakness be our boast,
And let us boast in You our Lord Jesus Christ.

My Psalm 143 – Despair and Anxiety

O Lord, why is my heart in despair?
Why am I imagining crazy things?
I am feeling anxious and uneasy,
About many parts of my life, O Lord.
I do not like these feelings at all.
They make me feel hurt and sinful.
Jesus, please turn this despair into joy,
And help me to praise You in it.
You know why I am feeling this way,
And You know what is wrong in me.
I trust You and You alone, my Lord,
For I know that I cannot trust myself.
Is this all my own spirit leading me?
Or is the enemy trying to pry me from You?
O Lord Jesus, is it my imagination,
That is bringing these ideas to my mind?
Am I leaving You out of my life's desires,
And am I sinning against You, Jesus?
Lord, I feel at times that all is against me,
That no one really knows me for sure.
It feels like they know my name only,
But they don't know the pain in my heart.
Lord, I want to give it all to You,
Because I cannot make it on my own.
For You are all loving and merciful, Lord!
You have put Your Spirit within me.
So why am I so anxious, in great despair?
And why can I not let You have it all?
Am I only trusting You with lip service?
Have I closed the door of my soul to You?

I know that You are there waiting for me,
To learn the lesson, You have planned.
I commit all my despair and anxiety,
I give it all to You, for Your destruction.
I trust You, Lord Jesus, with my heart and soul.
I trust You to help me through this time.
I want to serve You and You alone, Lord,
And put You on my heart's throne once again.

My Psalm 144 – You Are the Center of Life

Lord You are the center of life,
> You are the One Who holds it together.
> You are worthy of all our praise,
> You are worthy of all honor.
> Without You the world would collapse,
> For there is nothing that can take Your place.
> Man may think that he can replace You,
> And in his own power take full control.
> In his arrogance man says God is not real,
> And in his arrogance, he will die lost.
> Man thinks that he can do all things himself,
> But what power does he have to create?
> You are the Creator of the whole universe,
> And Your power keeps it moving.
> You spoke every little and being into being,
> And You made it perfect for us to live in.
> But it was man who brought on all the strife,
> All the pain and sorrow into this world.
> You are holy and righteous, man is not,
> And our tendency is to sin because of our nature.
> You, God, are sinless because of Your holiness,
> But man is born into sin by sinful parents.
> Man can be holy and righteous in one way,
> He must believe and trust in the Lord Jesus Christ.
> We are justified and sanctified by Christ alone,
> For none of our works or deeds can save us.
> Man's religions cannot save him in any way,
> Because rituals have no power to save.

Many are the lost who practice various religions,
But salvation comes through Jesus Christ only.
Help us to realize that we need You alone,
Not religious practices for salvation.
Let us know Your heart for our daily lives, O Lord.
And guide us into the plan that You have for us.
May each of us seek to serve You to Your glory,
Not out of selfish desires for gain but to Your praise.

My Psalm 145 – I Pray Only to You O God

You are my Lord and God,
>My Father in heaven above.
>I praise Your holy name, O Lord,
>And I seek to glorify You Father.
>You are the only true God,
>And the only One Who saves.
>O Lord God, please hear me.
>I pray that You will answer.
>I pray only to You for my need,
>For I know that You will listen.
>I can rely on You Father.
>For You are holy and righteous.
>You are Creator and Provider,
>And the only One Who did and can.
>You provided our way of salvation.
>You sent Your Son Jesus as a sacrifice.
>You made me into Your child,
>Because of Jesus's death on the cross.
>Lord God, You love us like no other,
>Seen through Your mercy and grace.
>You save us through Jesus Christ,
>And have given us gifts for Your glory.
>My Heavenly Father, You love us,
>When in our sinful state we are undeserving.
>I am thankful that You are my God.
>And I know what I have, and I am in You.
>I thank You O Lord for my eternal life,
>That I can have only through Jesus Christ.

For I know that I cannot save myself,
Because I am not holy, righteous, or good.
Lord God my Father I pray only to You,
Because You alone can answer prayer.
I lift my needs to You my dear Father,
Because You and You alone hear me.
My God, I worship You and lift my praise,
And I pray only to You because You are God.

My Psalm 146 – The One and Only True God for Me

Though my body aches a lot,
 And it is mostly wracked with pain.
 My Lord God, I will praise You,
 For You alone are worthy of praise.
 If ever I cannot praise You my Lord,
 I am sure that I will be in the grave.
 But then I have even more praise.
 Absent from the body, I will be with You.
 My body may be getting old and slow,
 But my spirit and soul are being renewed.
 Your Holy Spirit within me strengthens,
 And gives me new reasons to praise You.
 For You, O LORD, bought my soul from hell,
 And You saved me for eternity.
 It has cost me nothing to be Your child,
 But Jesus, it cost You Your life and Your blood.
 Who else could I praise for salvation?
 For it comes from only one name, Jesus.
 I have no reason to worry about anything,
 For You are my Protector and Provider.
 I have nothing to fear, even if this body dies,
 For my soul is saved for eternity long.
 I can have the confidence of my salvation,
 Because I know that Your promises are true.
 I praise You for Your holy word so powerful.
 And I praise You for salvation only from You.
 I praise You, Jesus, for our death on the cross,
 And I praise You for Your Holy Spirit, O LORD.

I praise You for Your holiness and righteousness.
And Your grace and Your mercies and love.
Without You in my life I am nothing but lost.
But You have given me life anew for eternity.
I love You, O LORD, my God, and Heavenly Father,
I need You, and I want You in my life each day.
For You are the One and only true God for me,
And my life is hidden in Christ with You, O God.

My Psalm 147 – Sometimes My Heart Grows Weary

Sometimes my heart grows weary,
    And my faith seems so weak.
    I doubt all that You've done for me,
    And my prayers are hard to speak.
    I can see my way to the holy altar,
    But my legs seem unable to go.
    In my heart I hear the Scripture.
    Your words of assurance let me know.
    When I feel too weak to stay in the fight.
    And I do not feel You are close to me.
    You are there to remind me Jesus,
    You won the battle and set me free.
    Remind me Lord to call on You.
    Please help my faith to be strong.
    May I always put my faith in You,
    For in the body of Christ I belong.
    My first call should be to pray.
    No matter what this life may bring.
    Lord, put the fire back in my heart,
    So, Your praise I will never fail to sing.
    For I have nothing to fear in You,
    Because in You my eternity is sealed.
    I praise You, Jesus, for dying for me,
    For in You salvation is revealed.
    O LORD, You are my Savior and King,
    For Your holiness and righteous I pray.
    Because in You, Jesus I'll be forever,
    In heaven for eternity, I will stay.

My Psalm 148 – We Need You Jesus as Our Savior

If a heart grows so weary,
>That the pain is in the spirit.
>And the soul is lost within itself,
>Because of the struggle within.
>The only way out is there for you,
>Trust in Jesus, His promises are true.
>Jesus is the answer for all your pain.
>But it may not be relieved so very quickly.
>He knows the hurt you have felt,
>And He knows every tear you've cried.
>Jesus is right there with you, my friend.
>It was for your every struggle that He died.
>Pain may change your outlook on life,
>But Jesus will change you from the start.
>The pain may not leave right away,
>But Jesus will be there with you every day.
>Jesus can help ease your struggles, friend.
>And help you see your life in a new way.
>Do not let your life's struggles get you down,
>But let the Strong One fight your battles.
>Give Jesus the deed to your problems.
>And let Him take them all away from you.
>There will still be times of pain and sorrow.
>You can have Him as Savior, tried and true.
>Jesus, please fight these battles.
>You are the only One Who can.
>Sometimes we are as weak as newborn babes,
>Even if it seems to make us look so strong.

We need You as our Lord and Savior,
To forgive and cleanse us when we do wrong.

My Psalm 149 – Never Let Us Forget to Praise You

You are my Lord and God,
>And You are my Savior.
>You have allowed me to be,
>And You have made me Your child.
>You are omnipotent, omnipresent.
>You are most holy and righteous.
>It is my honor to have You as my God.
>And it is my crown that You love me.
>My crown is the jewel of salvation,
>Through the Lord Jesus Christ.
>No other name has the power.
>And no other name can save us.
>Jesus, You sacrificed Your life for us,
>And we praise Your holy name.
>Your death allowed us to become.
>We have become children of God.
>Salvation brings us into eternity,
>For without You we are lost, O Lord.
>Help us Lord to desire You to be near,
>So that we will not forget You saved us.
>Lord Jesus, we need You every moment.
>Every moment of every day we need You.
>Help us to want all that You hold for us.
>Help us to remember we are Yours.
>Lord God, thank You for sending Jesus!
>Thank You for His death upon the cross!
>We praise You for sending Your only Son,
>To die in our place for all the sin in our lives.

Lord God, never let us forget our calling,
And never let us forget to praise You!

My Psalm 150 – My Life Will Begin Anew in Christ

I may not leave this world,
    With this old body alive.
    But I do know for sure,
    That when I do, I gonna fly.
    My life will change forever,
    In the twinkle of an eye.
    My true life will begin anew,
    When with the angels I will fly.
    My life may not seem like much,
    Because I don't own a lot.
    But my life is not made of things.
    I am completed by Who I've got.
    Jesus Christ is all I need in this life.
    I am not defined the things I don't have.
    For my life is found in Christ alone,
    And I don't need a lot of things.
    For even if this life gets me down,
    My heart is content because it sings.
    Jesus is my life, and He is my Savior.
    My life is hidden with Christ in God.
    The enemy cannot touch me now,
    For my salvation is eternal in Christ,
    Though this body may die and rot,
    My life has begun anew with Christ.

My Psalm 151 – Peace

My life has not been easy,
Not that I think it should be.
I have had my share of problems,
And had my portion of pain.
I am not complaining because,
I have peace I cannot explain.
For peace comes only from Christ,
Something the world cannot provide.
No matter what the circumstances,
I can have peace, yes great peace.
Because in Christ I have great peace.
It is a peace in God surpassing all understanding.
Even though the world may break me,
My spirit will live on for eternity.
Though this body may fail me, I know,
That this life is only my path to eternity.
Yes, though my body may be tired and weak,
The Spirit living within keeps me strong.
For the Holy Spirit made my heart His home.
And my heart will never more tend to roam.
And now I live according to the Spirit of God,
Not led about by every whim in my life.
For I gave Jesus control when I asked Him in.
And now I have a hope eternal that cannot die.

My Psalm 152 – Help Me with a Decision

I am in a quandary O Lord,
    And I am not sure what to do.
    I have a decision to make,
    And I do not relish its outcome.
    For no matter which I choose,
    People will be hurt and angry.
    O Lord, God, I need Your wisdom,
    To act on this decision, I must make.
    I am sure that You know how I feel,
    And I do not want to hurt anyone.
    I need Your guidance and wisdom.
    Please give me the words to say.
    Please, Lord God, help me to be.
    Help me to be open to Your guidance.
    Help me to hear Your words today.
    And help me to express them rightly.
    For You, O Lord are the Owner of wisdom.
    I am just a beggar asking for alms.
    You are the wisest in all the universe,
    For by Your wisdom, we were made.
    You, O Lord made us in Your image,
    And made us for fellowship with You.
    You are our Lord God of heaven,
    And You are Lord of this earth.
    I will praise Your name in all that I do,
    And I will praise You no matter what.
    I will glorify Your name in good or bad.
    No matter whether it means life or death.
    For I long to be with You, my Lord God,
    And with You, my Savior Jesus Christ.

Praise You, Lord for I know I can trust You,
Because I have no doubts that You are true.
Your holy word describes You as beautiful,
Showing Your power and majesty.
For You are Lord God, Jesus our Savior,
And You are the Holy Spirit in our lives.

My Psalm 153 – To Whom Can I Turn?

Dear Lord God, to whom can I turn,
    When life's struggles knock me down?
    Who can I talk to and share it in trust,
    When it seems as if all are out to get me?
    Why is it so difficult to find a good friend,
    When my life is on a downhill slide?
    The only one I can truly trust is You.
    O Lord God, You are my solid rock and savior.
    You will not fail me now or in the future,
    Because You are holy and just to judge.
    There is no way that You can let me down,
    But You may feel the need to chasten me.
    I know that I am a sinner, Abba, Father,
    And that I deserve much worse for all.
    You are a just God Who judges in holiness,
    But I was born in sin, and it lives in me.
    You know that man is a willful sinner.
    And that is why Jesus came to die for all.
    There are times that I feel as much a sinner,
    Just as much as You are holy and righteous.
    My sins burden me heart and soul, O Lord,
    But the sweetness of Your forgiveness soothes.
    I praise You that Your grace is abundant enough,
    For a sinner such as me is a total loss without it.
    Lord God, it is only because of Your love for man,
    And Your desire to fellowship with us we are saved.
    You sacrificed Your only Son, Jesus Christ for us,
    To give us the way to become righteous in Your eyes.
    You know that man's heart will lead him to sin.
    But Jesus death on the cross will lead us to You.

For You are the only one and true God, I know.
All other gods are made with man's hands.
They have no power or spiritual worth to us,
Just as there are many things that are god to man.
I praise You dear God, I love You and I need You.
I want You to be in my life each and every day.
For without You I would be just another lost soul,
Seeking for something that I cannot find myself.
True salvation comes through the Lord Jesus Christ,
And in Him alone is the way, the truth, the life found.

My Psalm 154 – Someone is Praying You Through

You ask the Lord, "Why me?"
    And feel lost and alone.
    You ask the Lord, "When O Lord,
    Will this pain be gone?"
    Your body is fighting you,
    And you cannot understand.
    Remember, someone is praying for you,
    You may find it hard to believe it's true.
    In all your pain and uncertainty,
    Look up, someone is praying you through.
    You may not see results right now but,
    Someone is fervently praying you through.
    You cannot find a reason for your hurt.
    You do not know if you did wrong.
    Someone may say "Confess your sins,
    They will be forgiven, and you will be healed."
    But you need to look to Christ our Lord.
    Ask Him to help you to understand.
    Keep in mind that others know you,
    They care deeply and pray for you.
    Out of the love for Jesus and you,
    These people are praying you through.
    It may not be pleasant or comfortable,
    They pray for you, praying you through.
    Place every care, hurt, and desire,
    Before our most loving Lord and Savior.
    Humble your heart before Him in love,
    And pour your heart out to him in prayer.

Trust in Jesus alone for the answer,
He knows that we are praying you through.

My Psalm 155 – My Pains do not Compare

O Lord You know how I feel.
    My body is wracked with pain.
    In many ways the pain is unbearable,
    And it seems my body is against me.
    I would seem that my body is revolting.
    And it is revolting against me.
    But on the days that it is at its worst,
    You are at Your best with me O Lord.
    You give me a peace that is unsurpassed.
    And You comfort me when I am in need.
    I know that You do care for me if I hurt,
    For You know the hairs that are on my head.
    Lord, please forgive me for feeling sorry,
    And complaining about my aches and pains.
    I have come to accept them as part of life,
    Just like the things that bring me joy.
    Because of You being in my life Jesus,
    I can rejoice even if the pain is too strong.
    Only You, Jesus can make a man feel well,
    And only You can make a man truly well.
    You can make life's struggles seem lighter,
    Because You love us body, soul, and spirit.
    I love You, Jesus Christ, I love You, Father,
    I love You; Holy Spirit for You loved me first.
    Lord, I know that I complain a lot about pain,
    But I am truly glad that I have it daily.
    I can rejoice in You when I'm in great pain,
    Because You suffered for me on the cross.

The pain and anguish You suffered for us,
Outweighs the aches and pains we suffer.
For God, You loved us enough to sacrifice,
Making Jesus the sacrifice for our sinful lives.
He became sin, the One who never sinned.
He died, bearing all of our sins Himself.
He suffered because He was separated from You,
His Heavenly Father so You would be ours too.

My Psalm 156 – Looking in the Wrong Place

I seem to be looking in the wrong place,
>For at times my mind goes looking.
>I do not know what I am looking for,
>Nor do I even know why I am doing it.
>I just lose track of where I need to be,
>Though not lost physically, but in thoughts.
>I know, Lord God, that I need to look to You,
>Because You are the answer to my searching.
>I know that in You I have no reason for doubt.
>And I have need of nothing else in my life.
>Jesus's death on the cross brought me to You.
>I am Your child because of His sacrifice.
>I need to look for the things that are true.
>I need to look for the things that are real.
>I need to see You in looking for truth,
>Not the world's idea of what is true.
>For I know that only You are the only truth.
>What the world has to offer is not close.
>Your truth provides all who believe with life.
>Life that is eternal through Jesus Christ.
>You are my Solid Rock, my Firm Foundation.
>The only one that I can completely trust.
>I know my life would be a void without You,
>Because a God shaped hole would be in my soul.
>I know that I need Your strength and truth.
>And I do not want anyone else but You Lord.
>You are the only One I need to look to,
>For You are the only One in Whom life is found.

I trust You Jesus, my Lord and Savior,
And I love You and not the things of the world.
Since my life here on earth is but a mere vapor,
I would be completely lost without You.
So why do I look, look for something unreal?
I believe that at times I do this to prove You.
I prove You, to my soul that I am lost,
Needing You every minute of every day.

My Psalm 157 – Lord God, I Need You Most of All

Lord, You are the God of my life,
>And there is no other God but You.
>You have met every need that I have.
>You met them before I even knew it.
>You O Lord, know more about me,
>More about me than I know myself.
>You purchased my salvation with Jesus's blood,
>For He was the sacrifice for my sins.
>I love You God my Father and God the Son,
>And I love You God the Holy Spirit.
>Because You, the triune God taught me.
>You taught me to love You and others.
>I am amazed by Your love and grace,
>Because You forgave me of all my sins.
>You did not forgive just the sins of the past.
>You will forgive all my sins every day.
>By Your forgiveness of my sin, I am made clean,
>Which is nothing any false god cannot do.
>I praise You for Your holiness and righteousness,
>For Your salvation, that I am made holy.
>I praise You for Your mercies new each day.
>I praise You for Your grace that is abundant.
>I praise You that You are a just and loving God,
>Who loves me in spite of my old sin nature.
>You are most holy in all that You do and say,
>For Your holiness will not let You be anything else.
>You are omnipotent, all powerful but loving.
>You are omniscient and omnipresent always.

You are Creator and a most honorable God,
And You are more powerful than all my sin.
I praise You for Your honor, majesty, and word,
For You have instilled in me the fruit of the Spirit.
I praise You for wanting me to be like You,
By endowing me with Your most holy gifts.
Lord, I praise You, I want You in my life.
I love You Lord God for I need You most of all.

My Psalm 158 – O Lord Jesus, You are all I Need

Lord as I walk through this life,
I will have many troubles and woes.
There will be times of great sorrow,
And there will be times of great joy.
Please help me during these times,
Though I may think am strong, I am weak.
Dear Lord, help me to focus on the need.
Help me to leave the want in the dark.
For You, O Lord, know the things I need.
And You know the things that I want.
Help me to see the things that I need,
More than the things that I think I want.
Though the things I want are not sinful,
They may not be profitable for me, Lord.
They may give happiness in short supply.
They cannot compare to the joy I have in You.
I do want to be happy but not at the expense,
Of losing the joy and love I have in You Lord.
You know me better than I know myself.
And You know that I could easily stray.
But You, O Lord, have provided me the Way,
Jesus Christ who is the way, the truth, and the life.
In You, O Lord, I have all that I will ever need.
And it does not matter if I be rich or poor.
I am like the farm animal standing at a fence,
Oftentimes thinking the grass is much greener.
I am glad that I have You to lead me to truth,
For I know that You are with me all the way.

So why is it that I desire worldly things?
Is it because of my old sin nature? I say yes.
For Jesus You overcame the lusts of the flesh.
And You overcame every sin the world offers.
You came to earth for a brief period of time,
But You stayed pure and holy and knew no sin.
You, O Lord Jesus, are all I need in this world,
For You defeated sin, allowing me to be saved.

My Psalm 159 – Lord God, I Need You

Lord God, I need You as always,
    But today I need You even more.
    I have done and said some things,
    That may be hurtful to some others.
    Sadly, the things that I said are true,
    For they came from Your holy word.
    It would seem that Your Scripture,
    Has cut them to the quick, to the core.
    Since Your word is so very sharp, Lord,
    Sharper than any two-edged sword.
    It has left them angry, and hate filled,
    Because the desire was filling the heart.
    It was what seemed to be the very best.
    The best thing for them at the time.
    Doing what was what seemed right,
    In their own eyes, not Yours, O Lord.
    The will is very strong but most sinful,
    For they justify the wrong that is done.
    Looking into their heart they see want,
    They want to feel good, not know the need.
    This one or that one may get the idea,
    But it is easily washed away by sin's thrill.
    The thrill of sin will last only a short season,
    But the joy we have in Christ is eternal.
    Please Lord God, let the joy of Jesus Christ,
    Fill and rule in their souls today and always.
    Help them to see the error of their ways.
    May Your word open their eyes to the truth.
    Send Your Holy Spirit to soften their hearts,
    And may they come to true, eternal salvation.

Open the hearts that have been filled with sin,
So that they will accept the truth of Jesus.
May they understand that life is only in Christ,
Because He was sacrificed for all of our sins.
May Jesus Christ rule in their hearts and souls.
May You be glorified through their salvation.

My Psalm 160 – This World is Turning Inside Out

The world seems to be turning inside out.
    Turning against itself and all who live here.
    The people are cheering evil and hating good,
    The truth is equally hated as are You, O Lord.
    Everyone has his or her own truth for life.
    And they have their own god that is not You.
    Lord God, I ask that You protect us,
    Those who are Your children by Jesus's death.
    For I can see that it is not too far off for us,
    To become even more hated by nonbelievers.
    We need You, O Lord God, to light our way,
    To know how we are to proceed in this life.
    Those who would seek to control our lives,
    Do not have You or Jesus as part of their plan.
    Their god has no power on its own without them.
    Their god is greed, selfishness, and divisiveness.
    They do not know You Lord but know You live.
    That is why they try to stamp You out of our lives.
    My prayer to You, O Lord God is that I remain.
    That I remain sold out for only You, not the world.
    I also pray that if persecution ever comes my way,
    That I will look to You for my strength and life.
    My life is not worth much to those of the world,
    Because they believe they have all the answers.
    To them no one who does not support their ideas,
    Is not worth having a life here on this planet.
    Many people have turned into haters of You, God.
    Thus, they have become haters of Your believers.

We have become the dregs of the earth, Lord,
And we are not worth the air we breathe to live.
Please dear Lord, let me be a brighter light to them.
Help me to be strong in my witness and my desire.
For I desire to glorify You in any way in which I can,
And it does not matter if the world likes it or not.
Please dear Lord, give me the boldness of the prophets,
So that my desire will be strong unto Your glorification.
And Lord, help me to present Jesus in love and grace.
Not worrying if my life is taken by those who hate.

My Psalm 161 – Within My Heart is Where You Are

I see You in all of Creation,
　　And I see You each day of life.
　　I know Your hands are on me,
　　For each day all I see is new.
　　In my heart and soul, I praise You.
　　Lord, I lift my hands up to You.
　　For Jesus, Your life paid my debt.
　　Your blood was shed for my sin.
　　And Jesus what was my worth,
　　That You would die for even me?
　　You suffered horribly on Calvary,
　　To set free the sinner like me.
　　You paid my debt upon the cross.
　　A debt that hung heavy over me.
　　You knew I could not repay You,
　　But my life, You made it Your own.
　　You loved me before I knew You.
　　How is such love You give so true?
　　My life, my heart, I give to You.
　　To whom else could I go but You?
　　There is no other Savior but Jesus,
　　And none so fair, holy, and so true.
　　For Jesus, You gave Your all for me.
　　So, Lord Jesus, I give my all to You.
　　I lift my hands up to You my Lord,
　　Jesus the only Son of God most high.
　　With joyful tears running down my face,
　　Your love and peace reign in my heart.

I raise my hands high in praise to You,
For from me You will never depart.
With my joy made full I reach to You.
I love You with all my heart and soul.
I reach out to Jesus; my need is strong.
And I reach up to You dear Lord Jesus.
I know I do not have to reach too far,
Because within my heart is where You are.

My Psalm 162 – Give Me Strength to Reach Out to the Lost

I love You Lord, O Lord my God.
I need You more now than ever.
Because this world is a real mess.
Sin runs rampant and no one cares.
Your holy word is wanted by no one.
All they can see is what they like.
O Lord my God, please help us.
The world is spinning out of control.
No one in this world can save us.
We need You to make us brand new.
The death of Jesus means nothing,
To a lost world drowning in their sin.
It is easier for the world to hate good,
And to revel in all their iniquities, Lord.
Because the truth never comes to mind.
They would not know it if it touched them.
All they want is to feel better themselves.
And it does not matter who they may hurt.
Lord God, we need Your very presence.
We need Your grace to flood the earth.
The world is beginning a large tailspin,
And it will crash with too many lost souls.
They need salvation from Jesus Christ,
By the blood He shed for each one of them.
Lord, You know the world is getting colder.
Every day many more will die needlessly.
Most sadly, they will die because of the lie.
They do not want to hear God's Own truth.

For them it is more pleasing to live in sin,
Not fearing the consequences to come.
O Lord God, we need Your Holy Spirit,
Come mightily upon and within our hearts.
Help us to desire to reach the lost souls,
No matter how much time or the cost.
God, please give me Your Spirit in power.
Give me strength to reach out to the lost.

My Psalm 163 – There is None Who can Compare to You

There is a light in the distance,
 Getting closer by the moment.
 The brightest I have ever seen.
 It is brighter than sunlight of day.
 It is coming from only one place,
 The Life, the Truth, and the Way.
 Oh, it is Jesus Christ our Savior,
 Who won our very salvation.
 He died on the cross to set us free,
 Gaining for us life of eternity.
 God sacrificed His only Son for us,
 To set our lost souls forever free.
 Praise the Lord for His salvation,
 Allowing us to join His family.
 Thank You dear Lord our God,
 For Your mercies and Your grace.
 You set us apart from the world.
 To be a part of Your holy place.
 We see how beautiful You are,
 Through the love You have for us.
 We see how You love us so,
 So much that Your Son died for us.
 How great the mercy and grace?
 How perfect the Savior Jesus Christ?
 How sinful are the men on earth?
 So sinful that we all deserve death.
 Praise You for allowing us to see,
 That You have a perfect plan for us.

O how much You love us as we are,
And continue to do so even in our sin.
O Lord God, my praise falls so short.
And how weak it is compared to Your love.
I would not be where I am today,
If I did not have You as my Lord God.
You are perfect in all that You do.
There is none who can compare to You.

My Psalm 164 – At Times, My Life is in Disrepair

At times, my life is in disrepair, Lord,
 And I know the reason why it is as it is.
 My life gets very hectic and listless,
 Because I have strayed from Your love.
 I know how this happens and why,
 Because I want to do it by myself.
 I know that You meet all my needs,
 And You know my needs before I do.
 You know each word that I utter.
 You know the love or despair within.
 My life is no secret to You, O Lord,
 For You know me better than I do.
 I cannot hide anything from You,
 Because my life is an open book to You.
 It does not matter if I hide in a closet,
 Or even in a cave because You see it.
 You do not invade my privacy, Lord.
 You respect it enough to let me err.
 I know that Your love protects me,
 Because You keep me safe from myself.
 You are able to urge me forward, Father,
 Even if I am struggling along in pain.
 And I thank You for loving me so much,
 That You even know my deepest hurt.
 You know my innermost thoughts, Lord.
 And You see the mistakes I can make.
 Please dear Lord, do not leave me alone,
 Because though I think I am smart, I'm not.

I may know how to do a lot of things,
But I am using the things that You created.
O Lord God, You are holy and righteous.
I am neither one when on my own, Lord.
You are all powerful and mighty to save.
I am easily led astray and lost in my sin.
You are loving and merciful to help me,
Find my way back into Your fold again.

My Psalm 165 – O Lord My God, I Can See Eternity

O Lord my God, I can see eternity,
    And I know it is coming for me.
    For Your promise is never too late,
    Because for You Lord God I will wait.
    I know that it will come when You say,
    And in my soul, I wait in awe of that day.
    For Your promises will never fail.
    I know that they never will.
    From the beginning You foretold the end,
    And all the unsaved to hell You will send.
    But those who know Jesus are not lost,
    Because with His life Jesus paid the cost.
    O Lord my God, I wait for that day,
    For in Your eternal fold, I do long to stay.
    For this life can come only through One.
    He is Jesus Christ Your only begotten Son.
    I praise You God my Father in heaven above.
    You are the Creator of eternal, lasting love.
    It is written in Your holy word that if I believe,
    And I know You are holy and cannot deceive.
    I trust in Your word in my heart it is stored,
    To renew my faith and my trust in You Lord.
    I know that it is not a lie and cannot ever be,
    Because I see all You have done for me.

My Psalm 166 – The Grief Comes in Waves Flooding Over Me

This death hit me harder than most.
    And I do not understand just why.
    Why did this friend have to die,
    And go home to be with You Lord?
    He leaves his loving family wondering.
    Why did this have to happen now?
    But I know he put his trust in You,
    And his faith was always so true.
    We all miss his presence here with us.
    It feels like a hole is in everyone's heart.
    The waves of grief flood over our hearts,
    And the tears of sorrow fall like rain.
    Although it may seem crazy for many,
    We know that we have only so much time.
    You are the one Who knows our lives,
    And how long we each shall live, O Lord.
    For Lord God in Your holiness, we agree.
    There is a reason we do not need to know.
    For if I knew my day and time, I would lose,
    The time I have with You, lost in years of sin.
    I would wait until the very last of my days,
    To commit my life to You for salvation.
    Thinking that I knew when I would die,
    Then I would have nothing to worry about.
    So, I praise You, O Lord, my God, and Father,
    For You know how many more are like me.
    I praise You for my eternal salvation in Christ.
    And I praise You for the life that I do have.

Because I know that I am much better off,
With my life hidden in Jesus Christ, my Lord.
Though I know that my life is complete in You.
It does not take away the grief and sadness.
For there is still a spot in my heart missing,
The one who came home to live with You.
By faith I live my life and give it all to You.
You are my Lord and Savior, one truly true.

My Psalm 167 – God Does Not Know a Stranger

In this world there is much chaos,
    And it is getting worse every day.
    Jesus is the last one they want,
    They want to live life their own way.
    They cannot see the truth, Lord.
    They want to live to be free to sin.
    They may say there is really no God.
    If there is, why does He let some die?
    If He is there, why does He not hear,
    The pleas of the sick and the dying?
    Is God real does hear my plea,
    Can He see my pain and hear me crying?
    God knows that people hurt and die,
    He knows when they hurt and suffer.
    Even though you do not believe in Him,
    He is still seeking to save you for eternity.
    Though to You, God may be a stranger,
    But you are no stranger to our Lord God.
    He knows all that You are going through.
    And He seeks after your heart my friend.
    You may not know Him, but He knows you.
    Again, to Him you are not a stranger.
    Though you may consider God a stranger,
    He knows you; you are no stranger to Him.
    God does not wish to see anyone perish.
    He wants us by our own will to trust in Him.
    He will not force anyone to accept Him,
    Or salvation through His Son Jesus Christ.

He wants us to come to Him as a sinner,
To be cleansed by the blood of Christ.
For Jesus freely died for the sinner.
He suffered more than we can ever know.
Jesus died on the cross as a sin offering,
Not despising the death that He died.
He did not die for the saved ones,
But he died for all who would come to Him.
He loved us enough that He gave His life,
To satisfy the holiness of a righteous God.

My Psalm 168 – Jesus Died for the Answers to Your Prayers

You may ask, "Why do I pray?
Is there anything in it for me?"
To which I would graciously reply,
I am not praying for only myself.
I am not looking to gain anything.
I pray out of the desire to help.
Prayer to me is something free.
The time I spend in prayer is good.
I pray for others because I care,
And I pray for them out of love.
My prayers for others are free.
But the answers cost Jesus His life.
I do not pray to receive a reward.
I love other people enough to care.
I care because Jesus told us to,
And I accept this commandment.
Ego and selfishness are not involved,
But the love of the Holy Spirit is.
It may seem strange that I do this,
But is just as natural as breathing.
I do not pray seeking things for myself.
I pray for God to touch people's lives.
I ask Him to heal their bodies of illness,
Or to help in a tough situation.
Answers do not always come as asked,
Because God knows our every need.
He knows what each person needs,
Before they know it themselves.

God is all knowing and all loving of us.
That is why He does answer our prayers.
You may say that "God has never answered,
The prayers that I have spoken to Him."
So, I ask, "Are you one of His children?
Is Jesus your Lord and Savior, my friend?"
"If you do not or will not trust our Savior,
How can you expect God to give what you ask?"

My Psalm 169 – Praise You Lord for Those Who've Gone Home

O Lord God, it seems that we have entered,
    Into a season of sadness and personal loss.
    Some of our brothers and sisters have gone,
    And they are now in Your holy presence.
    Our Father, we miss each one in our hearts.
    And we long to have them here with us.
    We know that You put them in our lives,
    To fill that very special place You saved.
    You, O Lord, know the pain we are feeling.
    But You also know the joy we have as well.
    For they are with You now for eternity,
    As a part of Your eternal, everlasting plan.
    Though the time seemed short to us now,
    You have blessed us with eternity and love.
    Maybe we missed telling someone, "I love you!"
    We can rest assured that we still have a chance.
    For a period of time our grief and sadness,
    Still come in waves and we may be gripped in fear.
    You, O Lord God, have promised us much more.
    For only You can give us peace of mind in love.
    We trust Your holy word and all its promises,
    Because we know that You are holy and righteous.
    Because of Your holiness You cannot lie to us.
    And we place our complete faith in You, O Lord.
    In time the tears may dry, and loss turns to hope.
    We can be strong because of You Lord God.
    Because You sent Your only Son, Jesus Christ,
    Who became the propitiation for all our sins.

Without Jesus's death on the cross we are lost.
But because of His shed blood we are redeemed.
For our faith in Him led us to our salvation, Lord.
And it is our faith that will lead us home to You.
Please Lord, accept our praise and thanks,
For allowing us to know and love those gone before.
For we know that we are saved by grace,
Through faith in Jesus Christ for all eternity.
And it is by faith that we can know in certainty,
That we will see each one of our loved ones again.
And it is all because You loved us enough, Lord,
To become the ultimate sacrifice for all who believe.

My Psalm 170 – We Praise You O Lord for We are Alive

O Lord God, we come humbly before You,
    In thanksgiving and praise for Your name.
    For You have met us where we are in need.
    And You have met each one of them, Lord.
    We rest assured that You know what our needs.
    For Your word says You know them before we do.
    We come before You with love in our hearts.
    And we come with awe and praise for You.
    Thank You for Your love and Your grace, Lord.
    And we thank You for Your mercy and love.
    We thank and praise You for our salvation,
    Bought with the shed blood of Jesus Christ.
    You, O Lord, are the Creator of the universe.
    And You are our Creator and our Father.
    In Your holiness and love for our souls,
    You created a plan for all who would believe.
    In Your holiness and righteousness, You did,
    What no man could ever do for us the sinner.
    We want You in our lives every day we live.
    We need You more than anything Lord.
    For we know without faith in You, our Lord,
    We have no way in which we can be saved.
    For us to have salvation we must have faith.
    And that faith must be in our Lord Jesus Christ.
    You seek to save us because You love us.
    And You want us to love You as You love us.
    You know that we are sinners from birth,
    But You still love us so much that You want us.

We know that You do not need us O Lord,
But You desire to have fellowship with us.
Please put in all our hearts the desire.
The desire to glorify You with our very lives.
We are but lost souls wandering in the darkness.
Without You, Jesus, we are lost for eternity.
We praise You Father, we praise You Jesus,
And we praise You Holy Spirit, for we are alive.

My Psalm 171 – Salvation Can be Found in Only One Name

I come humbly before You, O Lord,
> With praise and thanksgiving in my heart.
> For You, O Lord, are my holy Provider,
> Even though I may think I have a need.
> I do know that You provide for all I need.
> But You do not give all the things I want.
> You know my needs before I even do,
> And You supply them at the right time.
> I have no need of worry for anything,
> Even when I think that You do not hear.
> Though there may be a tiny seed of doubt.
> I know my worries are completely in vain.
> I thank You and praise You for my salvation.
> And I praise You for Jesus's ultimate sacrifice.
> Your timing for this event was perfect, Lord,
> Because You knew me before I was born.
> I praise You for Your holiness and righteousness,
> Your love, grace, and Your mercies new each morn.
> Jesus, You are most worthy of all my praise,
> And You are worthy of all my love and worship.
> As Your holy word says, You are worthy,
> For You are worthy to open the scroll.
> You are the Lamb of God, the holy sacrifice,
> Giving Your life freely for the lost.
> There is no magic formula for us to be saved.
> And it is not what we do or say that saves us.
> For we know that You are the way, the truth,
> And You are the life, the only way to God.

Salvation can be found in one name only,
That name is Jesus Christ, the Son of God.

My Psalm 172 – May there be a New Name in Glory

O Lord God may there be a new name in glory.
May You open the heart of my friend to You.
May I be ready to share Your love with him.
And may the Holy Spirit spice my words with love.
And dear Lord, please show him Your truth.
Let it show its holy, saving power to his heart.
Lord God may Your words fill my speech.
And may the beauty of Your love show through.
Please break down the walls of all resistance,
With Your love, Your mercy, and Your grace.
My prayer O Lord is that Your salvation plan,
Be as clear and powerful as the sun shines bright.
We all need a Savior in our lives, God our Father.
And You know that we need the Lord Jesus.
People need to know that Jesus is the only way.
For He is the way, the truth, and the life.
All other offer only lip service and lost eternity,
As they do not believe that Jesus is Lord and Savior.
O LORD God, You are so awesome in all Your ways.
You are the only holy, righteous, and true God.
You offer us life eternal through Jesus our Lord,
And it is free for the taking, if only we will take it.
We know that Jesus died on the cross for our sins.
Only Jesus could do that because He was sinless.
For He came to earth to live as a man in the flesh,
But unlike us He kept Himself holy and sinless.
Satan tried to tempt Him to worship him only,
And to worship him as if He were God Himself.

Jesus stayed true to His calling as the Lamb of God,
To die a horrible death that we might live with Him.

My Psalm 173 – God, I Trust You More than Before

Lord God, I trust You more than before,
For I know that You watch over me daily.
Your love and grace have made me whole.
And Jesus's death on the cross saved me.
I do not trust You because of what I see.
But I trust You because Your word is true.
Holy God my Father, You are righteous.
You are holy, loving, gracious and merciful.
Jesus You are my holy Savior and more,
And You intercede for us when we need You.
Holy Spirit, You are my guide in this life,
Sent by the Father to be our Helper in everything.
Jesus, your presence in my life defines me,
Because I long to serve and worship You.
Jesus, I would not be here today without You.
You saved me from my life made up of sin.
I would have no place to turn if not for You.
For salvation is found only in You, Jesus.
My life was as if beating my head against a wall,
And it was the same every day that I lived.
It was like being lost in a circular room,
The only way out was a door in the corner.
In other words, Jesus You are the door.
You provided me a way out of a sinful life.
All I can do now is praise Your holy name,
And I can shout it loud as I can for all to hear.
I love You Lord Jesus for You are my Savior.
I praise You Jesus for Your love and grace.

I want to share Your love and salvation.
Share it with the entire world for them to see.
Though some may hate or despise You Lord,
I can do nothing but praise Your holiness.
Those who say they hate You do not know You.
They do not know how much You love us.
My prayer and desire for them is to meet You,
And fall in love with You, Jesus my Lord, and Savior!

My Psalm 174 – Help Me to Reach Out to the Lost

Lord, I know that yesterday is gone,
  And that today is a brand-new day.
  But the enemy keeps reminding me,
  Of all the sins I committed years ago.
  I know that those sins were forgiven,
  When I accepted Your salvation plan.
  You, O Lord God, defeated the enemy.
  He has no power over my life.
  He may try to trick and confound me,
  But I am safe within Your fold forever.
  You have put Your Holy Spirit within me.
  He strengthens me when I am weak.
  I praise You Lord God for all You do.
  I love You more and more each day.
  I praise You Jesus for being the sacrifice,
  For my sins and the sins of the world.
  All they must do is to believe Your word,
  And accept the forgiveness of their sins.
  Please dear Lord, help me to reach out.
  Give me a desire to tell those who are lost.
  I want to tell them about Your great love.
  And why You died for their sins if they believe.
  Please dear Lord Jesus, spice my words,
  With Your love and grace for their salvation.

My Psalm 175 – I Am Free

My life was nothing but a mess.
And everything went so wrong.
Because I searched to be thrilled,
When all I needed was to be filled.
I wanted life to be like it was candy.
So, I let the world carry me along.
But nothing that I tried met my need.
My heart needed so much, much more.
The more I bought the more I needed,
For it was the world's call that I heeded.
I believed things would meet my need,
But only more sadness was in store.
The in desperation I called out in fear,
Because life must be more than this.
I cried out to the Lord, tears in my eyes.
"If You are real, please hear my prayer.
Please come into my life if You are real,
And let me know that You really care."
And then like a dove ever so gentle,
You came into my heart and now I see,
That I had searched the world for truth,
But I could not find it by any means.
And ever so gently You took my sin aside.
You cleansed me from sin, now I'm free.
Oh, Jesus, You removed me from death.
And You took away its victorious sting.
You changed me from the inside out.
You gave me a new heart that is alive.
Now I know that You are alive and real!
And my life has a brand-new song to sing.

Jesus, I do not know how I could doubt You,
Now that I know so very much about You.
Because of Your sacrifice unto death,
Gave my dead spirit and soul a new breath.
And I am bound by Your love for eternity,
Because by God's wonderful grace I am free.

My Psalm 176 – Jesus, You Came into My Life

Jesus, You came into my life,
>When all I knew was pain and strife.
>You made my heart Your forever home.
>You brought peace like I'd never known.
>You brought Your love for which I pined.
>For it is by Your will that, which I do find.
>God my Father Your holiness I desire.
>Fill my heart with Your Spirit's holy fire.
>I do not want to go through this life alone.
>It is for Your Holy Spirit mine does groan.
>For You are life and all it has to give.
>And by Your Holy Spirit I want to live.
>My life is brand new, made in whole,
>You came in and You saved my soul.

My Psalm 177 – Only You, O Lord Can Ease My Pain

There are days when life gets me down.
The pain in my body is ever present.
Sometimes I wonder in my sad heart,
"Lord, why me? What did I do wrong?"
And it becomes easy to feel so sorry,
Not because of sin but because I hurt.
O Lord, You know that I really love You.
And I place my full trust in what You do.
You promised that I would not be tested,
Beyond that which I can withstand by faith.
You are my strength and holy power.
You are my Savior and by You I can stand.
But Lord God, there are days I want to cry,
Because the pain is overwhelming to me.
Those around me give me much free advice.
I know that they mean well but make it worse.
You know Lord, there are many days I have,
When it is harder to find a spot without pain.
Many look at me as if I had committed a sin,
As to why I am hurting so badly from within.
They wag their heads as if to judge me,
Because I cannot do all the things as before.
I would not wish this pain on them O Lord,
Because it is my pain alone that they cannot see.
O Lord God, please forgive me if I do cry!
Cry out in pain and again ask You, "Why?"
Because every part of my life is affected.
And my heart grows weary trying to overcome.

Man's medicine cannot begin to ease the pain.
They serve only to dull the senses and thought.
You, O Lord, and You alone are my answer,
For in You alone, I can find peace and joy.
I can find no resolution in man's offerings,
For You are the True Healer and Great Physician.
In You alone, O Lord God, can my needs be met.
You are the Author and Perfecter of my faith.
I love You Lord God, You provide for me always.
I confess that I feel sorry for myself at times.
Thank You for sending Jesus to save me,
From my times of self-pity and for raising me up.
Only You can fill those painful holes in my life,
And soothe my pained and weary body and soul.

My Psalm 178 – Because of You

Lord God, I need You, I want You,
    I want You in my life every day.
    I love You Lord God, my Father,
    For You provided for my salvation.
    I praise You Lord for all that You are,
    For You are the one and only Creator.
    You are holiness embodied in One.
    You are still seated on Your holy throne.
    Jesus, You were the sacrifice for all.
    You died to save all who would believe.
    Holy Spirit, You indwell the saved,
    And You are all the triune God in One.
    Thank You that Your ways are not as mine,
    For my sinful nature seeks full control.
    My spirit is strong, but my flesh is weak,
    But when I am weak You make me strong.
    You make me stronger than ever before,
    I can be strong, and it is all because of You.

My Psalm 179 – You Humble Me by Simple Means

Lord, You humble me by simple means,
But You use it to hone me as a sharp knife.
You show me the errors of this life I live.
You discipline me for my sinfulness.
Though I may sin, You still love me the same.
Your love, O Lord, never grows tired or weak.
I have a proud mind and egotistical heart.
I like to think that I can do things myself.
Even though I know that I need You, I rebel,
For I am an impatient, moody type of soul.
Sadly, I know that I need to consult You first,
But I do not wait because I want it now.
But You, O Lord, know me better than myself.
You know what it takes to turn me back.
Sometimes You make something impossible,
But other times You let me learn by mistake.
You love me enough God to let me be wrong,
So that I will learn my lesson by my sinfulness.
The sad thing is that I know that You are there,
No matter how far I go from home or from You.
Even though I know that You are always with me,
I sometimes let myself believe that You are not.
I will then realize that it is me and not You,
Because I have turned my back on You, my God.
I know O Lord, You will help me to get back,
And that you will keep closer than I realize.
It is not that I want to run my life all by myself.
I realize that I truly need You but I'm selfish.

There are certain things I want all to myself,
And I know that I should share them with You.
I confess, Father God, I am a lowly sinner,
And that I am sinning against You in all of this.
My impatience and stubbornness are sinful,
Because I do not want to wait on You at times.
But I know that in the end, I come out the loser,
Because I do not come to You, first O Lord.

My Psalm 180 – Jesus, Your Love Took a Toll on My Heart

Jesus, loving You has never felt so good,
>   But at times it has never felt so bad.
>   It is not because Your love is not good.
>   It is not because You do not love me.
>   It comes from the sometime sadness I feel.
>   Because I have sinned and let You down.
>   Your love has taken a toll on my heart Lord.
>   You took away the life draining sin from me.
>   You paid the toll, the price for all my sin.
>   And You replaced the void with Your Spirit.
>   Your love is the least expensive of all,
>   But it cost Your life, for my life of sin and shame.
>   Your love is so new to me each and every day,
>   Just like Your mercies that are new every morn.
>   You removed my sinful desires out of love,
>   And broke my heart to repair it Yourself.
>   Jesus, I hate the sin that is in my life, my Lord.
>   I hate it because it causes You to hurt for me.
>   My life is so much more now than it used to be,
>   Because You live within me and lead me.
>   I have no reason to not trust You for everything,
>   Only my selfish desire to be in control does that.
>   Sin seems pleasurable for a short season, Lord,
>   But it hurts for a much longer time, I know.
>   Lord God, Father, Abba, I love You and thank You,
>   For You are my provider and my only God.
>   Jesus, You are my Lord, my Savior, and my All in All.
>   What or who else could I long for but You?

Holy Spirit, You are my Guide, my Intercessor in prayer,
You help me to love my triune God even more.
So why would I wonder, or why would I doubt?
You paid the ransom for my life and my soul.
Your blood washed away all my dirty sin.
It cleansed my soul and gave me a new life.
I want to glorify only You my one and only God,
For I am rich in Your love, grace, mercy, and holiness.

My Psalm 181 – Let it be for You O Lord

O Lord God, my Heavenly Father, my Abba,
    You are holy and righteous, You are loving.
    My life should be centered around You,
    But sometimes I let life get between us.
    I allow my focus to be taken off You, Lord,
    When my life should be all about You.
    I pray that my heart is in the right place.
    And I pray my life is going in the right direction.
    It should all point to You, Lord God, my Father.
    And it should be focused on Jesus as well.
    For without You Lord God, Jesus, Holy Spirit,
    Life is a waste and a lot of nothing to gain.
    Father God, You are my Provider, Protector,
    And You know each move I make and my thoughts.
    I know that You love and care for me Lord God.
    I know that I am saved, and my sin forgiven.
    You knew me before I even entered this world.
    I know that You loved me before my life began.
    I know that I am a sinful man, saved by Your grace,
    Clinging to Your mercies that are new every morn.
    I confess that I am a sinner, living in sinful flesh,
    But I know that I am forgiven by my faith in Christ.
    My soul would be lost for eternity in the lake of fire,
    If it was not for Jesus's death on the cross for my sin.
    I praise You for Your plan of salvation, free for me.
    My salvation cost me nothing, but Jesus paid it all.
    Lord God, may I be humble when I come before You,
    With no pride or selfish desires for only myself.
    May I always put others before me and my wants.
    Help me to fill their needs through Your grace.

As some may say, "I was once was dead but now alive."
I am alive only through Your grace, mercy, and love.
You have met all of my needs and some of my desires.
And You had a plan to use them to Your glorification.
Lord God, may my life be lived for You and You alone,
No matter where I am or what I may do, let it be for You.

My Psalm 182 – For All Eternity

My life is nothing to be envied,
But I love it because of who I am.
It is not simple from day to day,
For it can get complicated in a heartbeat.
I am thankful that I have a helper.
One Who is not seen but o so powerful.
I thank You Jesus for being in my life,
And for the Holy Spirit living within me.
Though life may be hard to live,
I can turn to You in my times of need.
You came into my life when I asked.
Your Helper, the Holy Spirit came too.
For those days when I feel lost and sad,
I can always rely on You, Jesus, for love.
The love You have for me and all the saved,
Is eternal and will be with us forever.
I do not have to seek to find You Lord,
Because You are always there for me.
Your promises are always the truth,
None of them have ever failed us.
You died a most horrific death on the cross.
Your own Father could not look upon you.
You Who knew no sin became sin itself,
As the sacrificial Lamb of God, the Father.
I cannot praise or thank You enough.
I can sing worship songs and praise You.
I cannot shout loud enough to share Your love,
But I can tell people I see about You Jesus.
My life changed for the better because of You,
And it is not because of my lowly stature.

Jesus, You make all things new in life,
Because You fill the void in each heart.
You died to save us from our horrible sins.
You bore them as You died on the cross.
For Jesus, You paid my debt to Your Father,
So that I may be with You for all eternity.

My Psalm 183 – You are the Only One Who Can Help Me

Why do my heart and soul feel so lost,
When I know You are right here with me?
How can these feelings creep in so freely,
When I have no reason to feel this way?
O LORD, my God, my Savior, and salvation,
You know what I am going through right now.
My whole faith is based on Your promises,
Written in Your Book of Books, Your Holy Word.
Those promises are true, whole, and complete,
Telling me that You are with me no matter what.
Though I am lost in a sea of pain and regret,
I know that You have not failed me yet.
Lord, O Lord what is it that I am missing now?
How do I get to where I need to be from here?
Is there a sin I have forgotten to confess to You?
Or am I being taught to trust You even more?
No matter what it may be, my faith is in You,
Because You are the one and only true God.
Your holiness and righteousness can make me,
More like You each and every day of my life.
By Your power and grace, I am given new life.
Praise You, that new life comes from Jesus Christ.
Please, my Lord, keep me from failing You.
You make me stronger than I can ever be.
By Your grace I am saved through faith in You
And by Your blood I am washed clean of sin.
I know that Your Holy Spirit resides within me,
Because He moves me to praise You each day.

So why do I have these days when I feel lost,
When I have You in my life only a prayer away?
No matter what I go through or how I may feel,
You are my Rock, my Salvation, and my Deliverer.
I can be strong in my weakness and my failures,
Because I know that You love me no matter what.
You, O LORD, are the only One who can help me,
For You are the one and only Holy, Most High God.

My Psalm 184 – We Love You God, Jesus, and the Holy Spirit

O LORD, my heart is in the pit of despair,
    I do not understand why it happened.
    I am not in despair for myself, O Father,
    But for people who are close to me, Lord.
    I know that in Your infinite wisdom Lord,
    That You know what is needed by all.
    We are Your children, Your very creation.
    And we are sometimes weak and burdened.
    I know that the people of whom I speak,
    Are feeling a deep burden of pain and loss.
    Why is it that their unborn child did not grow?
    And why did it have to happen to them?
    Although I do not understand "Why to them?"
    Did this sad loss have to occur now?"
    They already had a season of pain and sorrow.
    When it seemed that all between them may be lost.
    You brought her through a devastating illness,
    To become a healthy, lovely, loving woman again.
    But You in Your wisdom and discernment Lord,
    Had a reason that this child may not be born.
    To doubt Your reason may truly be a sin,
    But to try to understand why, may be life changing.
    The love for You has not changed nor has it faded.
    But the pain of the loss is something that You know.
    Please forgive any bitterness or anxiety that remains,
    For the blame is not placed on You Father or her.
    This kind of loss does not have a reasonable answer.
    At least nothing that is honest or true in this life, O Lord.

The truth that remains is that You love us enough,
To sacrifice Your only begotten Son for our sins.
Praise You Lord God, for Your eternal love for us!
That You loved us enough to want us as Your children.
You are holy and righteous, and You are infinite Lord.
There are no bounds or borders to keep Your love away.
Lord God, in and through our pain and deep sadness,
We love You, Jesus, and the Holy Spirit and praise You.

My Psalm 185 – Your Beauty is Found in Eternal Love

O LORD, Your beauty is always reflected.
It stands within my sight each day I live.
I do not see it in the things made by man,
But I see it in all of Your natural Creation.
Man's creations may outwardly be beautiful.
But they depend on things You have made.
I know that in my strongest of moments,
That I can never create anything of detail.
Your creation has Your mark on each one.
And it goes down to the most minute detail.
Man allows himself to be proud of his work,
Taking credit where it should be given to You.
For Lord, You created man and his intellect,
Giving him talents to use his knowledge.
Many men believe You were created by man,
And that You do not exist or have substance.
They give credit to coincidence or chance,
Because they cannot accept Your reality.
I place all my faith in You my Lord God, no other.
I know that all I am is only because of You.
Everything within me that is good is from You,
Because I was born a sinner without life.
But You sent Jesus to die on the cross for me,
Even for all who would believe in Jesus Christ.
You are my Creator, the only one and true God.
Our God who loved us enough to sacrifice Jesus.
Jesus became sin and paid our debt eternally,
And with His blood He bought our salvation.

The cost for us was our faith in Him, O Lord.
The cost for Jesus was His very own life.
There is no other god and no other thing,
By which we can receive eternal life, Lord.
There is no other god or idol to save our soul.
Only the Lord Jesus Christ, faith in Him saves us.
So, Lord God, Your beauty is beyond all compare,
Because in Your beauty we find eternal love.

My Psalm 186 – Your Message of Salvation

Lord, You know that there is a war going on.
It is all around us and many are sadly losing.
We sometimes go out without protection,
Leaving Your armor behind as we go on.
We are taking a stick to a battle a strong foe,
Who is armed with lies and many falsehoods.
How can I warn these people to put on the armor,
And make sure that they cinch it up tight?
Have we become a church like that in Laodicea,
That You warned that You would spit them out?
Why can they not see that they need Your word?
They need it every day of their life to be safe.
The salvation that many of us sought from You,
Has been forgotten due to the love of the world.
You still love us enough that You look out for us,
And supply all that we need to live this life.
It is Your desire that our lives be lived for You.
So, we need to rekindle that fire of love for You.
Men are seeking momentary satisfaction,
And instant gratification for the lust of the eyes.
It does not matter if the desire of their very heart,
Is here today and gone tomorrow, for they want it.
Their desire for You Lord God and Jesus Christ,
Has been replaced by getting the latest new thing.
How much longer are You going to let this go on?
And when will this sinful sadness come to an end?
Lord, please light the fire of desiring You only.
And use me however You find that I am best suited.

I am just a man by appearance, but I have Your Spirit.
You have given me gifts to glorify You to the world.
Lord God, Lord Jesus, I ask for a great revival for myself,
Not for myself alone, but that I have a stronger heart.
I desire to be stronger in my spirit and my love,
So that I can go into the world to share Your love.
Place in me anew, Lord, the desire to glorify You,
That Your message of salvation would be heard.

My Psalm 187 – Faith in No Other

O Lord, hear my plea so soft.
    Please keep my faith strong.
    May my spirit be of strength.
    So, Lord, that I will do no wrong.
    O Lord may my words ring pure.
    And may my faith always be sure.
    Because Lord, You're faithful to me,
    Just like You said that You would be.
    Father, You will never let me down.
    And You promised I'd get a crown.
    As long as my faith is in only You,
    As long as it would always be true.
    I haven't a lot of riches of my own,
    But my treasure is hidden in You.
    For You died, Lord, to save my life.
    And I believe every word is so true.
    For Your promises are good as gold.
    My faith in You will never get old.
    May my desire be only for You,
    That I would praise You each day.
    And my heart will never grow cold,
    For You will be with me all the way.
    Jesus, You won't leave me behind,
    Because in You, salvation I find.
    Jesus, may my thought be so pure,
    If not, may Your love be my cure.
    May live each of my days for You,
    To share Your salvation so true.
    O Lord, please help me I do pray,
    In Your loving arms I want to stay.

For Lord God, You are my Father.
I place my faith in You, no other.
Jesus, I love You more than my life.
Your love brought me through strife.
Holy Spirit, You are always my Guide.
Your leading is completely true and tried.

My Psalm 188 – My Every Breath Should be Praising You

O Lord, my eyes see Your beauty,
    And my heart and spirit feel it.
    I see Your work in all of Creation.
    And I see it in this body of mine.
    You have allowed me to be in pain,
    But You are always there for me.
    I have days that I hurt so bad, Lord,
    That every move I make is painful.
    You promised that I would be tested,
    But not so much that I cannot withstand.
    Some days I feel as if I might be there,
    That I have reached my breaking point.
    But then I remember You, O Lord,
    Nailed to a cross, severely beaten.
    You were beaten and scourged,
    Before You made the ultimate sacrifice.
    When I praise You for this, O Lord,
    My pains do not seem to be so bad.
    Pain seems to rule my life some days,
    But You are still sitting on the throne.
    Worries all but fade away when I see,
    You hanging there on the cross, Jesus.
    You died for me and all of this pain.
    Pain sometimes causes me to be distressed.
    All I need to do is focus my spirit on You.
    Claim the promises You made to believers.
    On those days when I do hurt so bad,
    I need to turn to You for comfort, strength.

You are there for me to see me through.
You care about me no matter how I am.
All my praise belongs to You Lord Jesus.
I sing my songs of love and praise to You.
When I lift my praise to You my Lord God,
I am lifted up in worship and love for You.
May Your praise always be on my lips,
For my every breath should be praising You.

My Psalm 189 – My Only Hope

O LORD God, my Heavenly Father it is You.
It is You and Your only Son Jesus Christ.
For it is only in You Father, You Son,
And Holy Spirit that I can find any kind of hope.
All of my hope is based on You the Triune God.
Father, Son, and Holy Spirit are the basis of my faith.
I know that my hope is not in vain and not lost.
It is not wasted as it would if I loved a rock.
Rock, wood, and metal are Your creations.
What can they do for me and where is the hope?
Why should I worship that which You created,
Rather than You, O Lord God, my holy Creator?
You have provided me and all who would believe,
A way to overcome death and separation from You.
For separation from You is the second death.
It's in the lake of fire that will burn, and not consume.
It is where the lost souls of man will remain eternally,
With no way to cross the greatest chasm of all.
My Hope is in You, Jesus, my Lord, and Savior.
For You became the satisfaction of God's holiness.
You are the propitiation for my life's sins,
Those past, those present, and for all time.
This is my hope that is in and through You, Jesus,
For You are my Lord and Savior for all eternity.
You did not hesitate to accept the punishment,
That should have been mine all alone, Jesus.
You love us enough that You would die for us,
Even though You did not need to Lord Jesus.
You gave me the faith and the hope in You,
That one day I can bow down before You.

Lord God, my Heavenly Father, I praise You,
For allowing me to be part of Your eternal family.
For You loved us enough that You made a sacrifice,
Of Your only Son so that whoever believes is saved.
All praise, glory and honor are Yours our Lord God,
For You are holy, righteous and You love us.

My Psalm 190 – You Are the Most Loving Savior and God

There is a time to shout out our love,
>   And there is a time to share it quietly.
>   There is a time to share all of our love,
>   And a time that it should be evident to all.
>   It is now my time to let people know.
>   Just how much I love You, Lord Jesus.
>   You were not quiet or shy about Your love.
>   Jesus, You shared it with the whole world.
>   You spoke the truth to many unbelievers,
>   And they thought You were possessed.
>   You knew exactly how they would react,
>   As You came as the loving Lamb of God.
>   I can understand how the people felt.
>   They heard something new and exciting.
>   But the enemy kept them from believing,
>   And accepting the free gift You offered.
>   I could have been right there among them,
>   Calling You horrible names and cursing You.
>   But You had a plan for my life before time.
>   You knew me from eternity before I lived.
>   You had a roadmap for my life before birth,
>   And if I accepted it, You would bless me.
>   Your love for me and all believers was proven,
>   When You gave Your all and became sin for us.
>   Jesus, Father, Holy Spirit, words cannot describe,
>   All You have given and done for the sinners.
>   I can see my life set out before me eternally.
>   I get a glimpse of what is ahead when I see You.

Though I do not see You standing in front of me,
I see the evidence that You are right beside me.
I praise You, O Lord for Your glorious majesty,
And Your holiness and righteousness so lovely.
I praise You for Your power, Your omnipotence,
For You overcame the power or death and grave.
You are the most holy of heaven and earth,
And You are the most loving Savior and God.

My Psalm 191 – Hate the Deeds Not the Person

My Father, my Heavenly Father,
    I come to You in sadness and despair.
    I do not understand why this happens,
    But I do know that it is very normal.
    Why should one country take over another?
    Who gives them the right to do this?
    Maybe this is part of Your great plan,
    That different countries pull together.
    I can see that You know what is happening,
    Because I believe that Your word is true.
    I praise You, Lord God, You are truly God,
    And You will keep it all in holy order.
    What I feel is not holy or righteous.
    What I think is not good or beneficial.
    My anger and my ire are a bright flame,
    That may show more brightly than my love.
    It seems that hatred for what is happening,
    Is not for the deeds done but those doing them.
    Lord God, please help me to understand.
    Help me to love those who I seem to hate.
    Lord, I need to remember You are in control,
    And that You are still sitting on the throne.
    What we are witnessing now could only be,
    The birth pangs of this world we live in.
    Lord, as was written, help me change that.
    That which I am able to change, nothing else.
    O Lord God, help me to seek Your glorification,
    Even though the world is becoming more evil.

I need to love and not hate because deeds are done.
I need to pray for salvation and not judgement.
For Lord God, You are the power and love,
The glue that holds the world together.
Please help us to come together in Your Name,
And to rely on You and not our own wisdom.
For true wisdom comes from You alone, Lord,
And true love is what You give us in this life.

My Psalm 192 – I Did Not Come Before You Humbly

I did not come before You humbly,
But I came to You out of my humiliation.
I could not see my way to You, Lord.
For I despised everything about You that I could see.
But with my heart broken in pieces,
Tears rolling, I finally came to You, O God.
It was like reaching up to touch bottom,
With the lowest part being out of reach.
But then I fell on my knees unto You,
And You reached down to pull me up.
And I understand now that You love me,
Even though I really do not know why.
I think of all the crude words I said,
Not knowing that I would need You.
I fell head over heels into the trap,
Set for me by Satan, the enemy.
I thought that feeling good was the best,
Not realizing his best was the very worst.
Now I have given my heart to You, Jesus.
For Jesus, You are my life and my strength.
I trust no other for eternal life but You,
For I know the promise is completely true.
You shed Your blood on the cross for me,
So that I could be clean and saved eternally.
Jesus, how could You love the wretched me?
Yet, You want me to be with You for eternity.
I know that Your love is true, and it is strong.
For no other can love me as much as You do.

Jesus, my heart I give to You, my Savior.
Now my soul is Yours forever and always.
Jesus, You shed Your blood for all of my sins.
Lord, You paid my debt with Your own life.
There is no man who can save the lost souls.
It can be accomplished only through You.
For You paid the ransom for my life and soul,
Setting me free of sin making me a child of God.

My Psalm 193 – I Am a Sinner

I come to You in awe this morning,
For LORD God You are most holy.
My heart yearns to see You eternally.
I want to be with You face to face.
I have nothing to hold me here.
In this world of pain and sorrows.
You, O LORD, have given me life.
A life free of the constant longing.
Your love has satisfied my desire,
And Your grace has set my soul free.
You, O LORD Jesus, suffered for me,
Because You love me enough to die.
Jesus, I believe that I am willing to die.
But when I think about it, am I ready?
Will my heart be true to Your calling?
Will Your name be the last word I say?
I want to serve You more than anything.
So says my heart and soul Lord Jesus.
You, O God know me better than I do.
For You have supplied each of my needs.
I am thankful that You meet my needs.
For my desires may lead me astray.
You can turn the dark into a new day.
But I can turn it back to dark with sin.
You, LORD God, are most righteous,
And You are the most holy of all.
You created the world where I live Lord.
You desire me to love and worship You.
You do not even need me, but You love me,
Even when I turn to go my own way.

I can often fall into sin if I drop my guard.
But Your Holy Spirit is there to remind me.
In my heart I know it is wrong to sin.
But I can lose easily and fall into that sin.
Lord God, I confess that I am a sinner.
I ask for Your forgiveness and cleansing.
I ask these things in Your Son's holy name.
I ask it all in the name of Jesus Christ.

My Psalm 194 – Have I Sinned Against My Brother?

O Lord, my thoughts are running wild.
My anger seems to ebb flow on its own.
I feel as if a brother has offended me,
And I plan to tell him what I really think.
I remember a prior hurt that he brought,
And it only fuels the fires of my distress.
Lord God, please help me give this up.
I know that it is not how You want me.
I am one of Your children, called a saint.
But I am afraid that I am not being holy.
I am concerned that my work be for naught,
And that I have wasted my time doing it.
O Lord, help me to see what I need to do.
Open my eyes and heart to Your leading.
Father God, help my blind eyes to see.
See the truth in this whole matter, Lord.
O Lord God, am I the one who is wrong?
Am I the one who has caused this, Lord?
If I have been unkind or underhanded,
Help me to have Your eyes to see it.
I do not want to have caused a division.
If I have done wrong, I will confess it.
May my heart be contrite if I am guilty.
Help me to have the right words to say.
O Lord God, I give this situation to You.
I admit I may be wrong and maybe sinned.
Father God, give me the desire to go.
To go to my brother to help ease the pain.

Lord, this is a painful situation for both.
We have a misunderstanding between us.
O Lord, please give us both hearts of love.
Help us to forgive each other no matter what.
May there be reconciliation in Your name, Lord.
And may it be healing of all wounds inflicted.
Father God, we are Your children by adoption.
You are our Father as if we were Your Chosen.
Lord God, I come to You, my Father, humbly.
I come humbly, with a contrite heart O Lord.
For You are our God and Heavenly Father.
We were saved by the shed blood of Jesus Christ.

My Psalm 195 – I'd Rather Fall Into the Arms of My Savior

I'd rather fall into the arms of my Savior,
    And be able to look at Him in His love.
    I do not want to fall into the arms,
    Of a most holy and righteous God of all.
    I want to be with Jesus for all eternity,
    And worship Him and our Father God.
    O Lord, Jesus You became the sacrifice,
    For all who would believe in You O Lord.
    You paid the debt for our sins on the cross.
    Your life You gave and only You suffered loss.
    Now I am free from the weight of my sin,
    And I can now see my future is so bright.
    Yes, I'd rather fall into the arms of Jesus,
    My Lord and my Savior Jesus Christ.
    I want to live in Your love and righteousness,
    So, I can come to the Father by Your love.
    Thank You Jesus that You love us as You do,
    Knowing that we were sinners without hope.

My Psalm 196 – Jesus Bought Me for Eternity

O Lord, my Father and God,
>When I pray what do You hear?
>Do You sense the tremble within?
>Do You know just what I fear?
>In my heart there is so much pain.
>O Lord, please do incline Your ear.
>If there be anything, any sin stopping You,
>From listening to my prayer, convict me.
>Please forgive me, do not hold it against,
>And please hear my most urgent cry.
>For without Your hand in this matter,
>I have no one else with which to share.
>Lord God, You alone are holy and righteous.
>Only You alone can know what is needed.
>You alone are God, and none can compare.
>For it is You, on Your holy throne are seated.
>Your love and Your power alone are strong.
>It is because of Your love that sin is defeated.
>O Lord, my Father and God, to You I pray.
>When I pray what do You see? What do You hear?
>Do You see my soul tremble within me,
>Or do you see my spirit eternally free?
>In my heart and soul there should be no doubt,
>For through Jesus salvation came to me.
>There is only one true Lord and God,
>And He is You so holy and so true.
>Jesus is the only way for us to be saved.
>For His death paid our debt for all eternity.

Yes, O Lord our God and Heavenly Father,
Your Son, Jesus bought me for eternity too.

My Psalm 197 – You are the God of Miracles

O LORD God, I come humbly to You.
My heart is sad and heavy with despair.
Father, who else can I turn to at this time?
That is why I come only to You in prayer.
I come to You Lord God and You Jesus.
Because I know that You truly do care.
Lord, my heart is aching for the only son.
And my heart is aching for the parents too.
I have felt the sense of loss and sadness,
That comes from the pain running through me.
It is as if a sword has pierced my inner parts.
It opens a wound I cannot heal without You.
So where can I go but before You on my knees.
I have no answer for my child's agonizing pain.
I know that this disease is not a chastisement,
But it comes because of sin's original stain.
So, in faith, love and hope I come to You, my Lord.
For only in You O LORD can my trust remain.
Jesus, I know You understand my deep despair.
You witnessed it in people when You were here.
You know the deep and abiding love they have,
That any parent has for a child they hold so dear.
That is why I ask You, O Lord, our Father in heaven,
Please ease the pain, comfort, and remove the anxiety.
Please O LORD God, may Your healing touch remove,
May it completely heal the body of this disease,
Touch and heal this child of these parents O Lord.
He is also Your child and I beg of You Lord, please.

May You be glorified by whatever Your will might be.
And LORD, hear the prayers lifted while on our knees.
We ask that as You hear our prayers lifted to You,
Asking that Your will be for a complete and pure healing.
LORD may Your answer be according to Your will.
It is our desire for a miracle to be Your love revealing.
We know Father You are the only God, our Abba.
We pray for him to be a miracle as we are kneeling.
We lift this up to You in the name of Jesus Christ,
Our Lord, our Savior, the risen Lord, our King.

My Psalm 198 – My Sacrifice of Praise

My heart is in my hands, Lord.
I give it completely to You.
My life is in great turmoil.
You are the only answer for me.
Every turn that I take is wrong.
There is always something in my way.
You make my paths straight Lord,
When I try to take every detour.
You can break my heart for Yourself.
The pain lasts only a short time.
You know me Lord, better than I do.
And You know my needs before I do.
It is extremely easy for me to detour,
And take the highly beaten path, Lord.
I see the struggles in the narrow way.
But I am gleefully blind in the easy path?
I know that You are with me always,
But I find it easy to stray from You.
You proved You love me, Lord God.
For You sent Jesus to die for my sins.
You are holy, righteous, and loving,
Even when I turn away from You.
Jesus, You died in my place for my sin.
Why can I not be willing to live for You?
O Lord, God You are clothed in holiness.
Your righteousness is unequaled, Father.
You are beyond all reproach by man.
And Your grace is offered freely to all.
You are all that this world needs, God.
For You are our Creator and Provider.

I trust You Lord God, You are my Father,
You are my loving Abba in heaven.
I need You in my life each and every day,
And each minute of every hour I live.
I praise and love You Father and Jesus,
And I praise You for Your Holy Spirit.
You are the Great Three-in-One God.
I lift my sacrifice of praise only to You!

My Psalm 199 – Cleanse Me and Make Me Whole

Why do I feel as if love left me?
    And why do I feel so empty?
    My life seems to have made a turn.
    And it seems to be for the worst.
    My soul feels as if it is burning,
    Burning with a desire I cannot fill.
    You know, Lord God, what I need.
    Only You can provide for it all.
    The world is trying to pull me back,
    By pulling on my soul for sinfulness.
    For Lord, I know why I feel emptiness.
    It is because I had a season of sin.
    Lord God, my Heavenly Father, it is You,
    Who are the only one who can save me?
    My spirit seems strong, but my flesh is weak.
    But it has been so easy to leave Your fold.
    I cannot do this all on my own Lord.
    I need to return to You in renewed faith.
    Lord Jesus, You are my Lord and Savior.
    You are the only One who can save me.
    For You conquered death and the grave.
    You rose to eternal life as Lord and King.
    I need Your Holy Spirit to be my guide.
    I need Him to guide and direct me, Lord.
    God the Father, God the Son, Holy Spirit,
    I need You in my life every day I live.
    I want Your love, care, and guidance.
    I need them each day that I might live.

Though You may chasten me Lord God,
And though it may hurt, it is for the best.
I confess that I need and want You Lord,
Back on the throne of my weary heart.
I confess that I have had sin in my life.
That sin in no way glorifies You Lord.
Please forgive me for my sinful ways.
Cleanse me completely, make me whole.

My Psalm 200 – Are My Prayers Empty Words?

O Lord God, do You hear my prayers to You?
Is there a reason that You might not listen?
Am I a loser or a terrible sinner who's lost?
Have I built a wall between You and me?
Is there an unconfessed sin that it in the way?
Is that sin preventing You from hearing my cry?
Lord God, You are most powerful in love,
And You are the most faithful of all.
I know that You love me even though I sin.
For You sacrificed Your only Son for my sins.
I also know that You may not listen to my prayers,
If there is sin that is standing between us.
Sin serves as a separation between me and You.
Lord God, help me to see what causes it.
May Your Holy Spirit convict me in my heart,
So that I can come before You clean in my soul.
Lord, I know that I have sinned against You.
I want to confess all my sins that I have missed.
You are the only One Who can forgive me.
You are holiness, righteousness, and Creator.
I need You in my life daily, every minute,
And I want You to be the Lord of my life.
You are the Lord God, the most holy of all.
You are my Heavenly Father, I love You.
Please Lord, forgive me of my sins against You.
Lift me up so I can stand in holiness before You.
I do not want my prayers to be empty words,
That You do not hear for I have sinned against You.

You O Lord are the only One I truly need,
You are life, love, and my loving Savior and Creator.

Page of **89**

About the Author

I began writing psalms in mid-2019. I was searching for commentaries and/or studies on psalms and found a couple of sites that featured instructions on writing psalms. I got hooked.I am working on more psalms and by the end of the year I hope to have 5 volumes of 100 psalms each.

About the Publisher